The Divided Soul

The Divided Soul

A Kierkegaardian Exploration

CLIFFORD WILLIAMS

WIPF & STOCK · Eugene, Oregon

THE DIVIDED SOUL
A Kierkegaardian Exploration

Copyright © 2009 by Clifford Williams. All rights reserved. Except for brief quotations in critical publications or reviews, no part of this book may be reproduced in any manner without prior written permission from the publisher. Write: Permissions, Wipf and Stock Publishers, 199 W. 8th Ave., Suite 3, Eugene, OR 97401.

Wipf and Stock Publishers
199 W. 8th Ave., Suite 3
Eugene, OR 97401

www.wipfandstock.com

ISBN 13: 978-1-60608-735-0

Manufactured in the U.S.A.

Quotations from Soren Kierkegaard's "An Occasional Discourse" are taken from Kierkegaard's *Upbuilding Discourses in Various Spirits*, edited and translated by Howard V. Hong and Edna H. Hong. © 1993 Howard V. Hong. Reprinted by permission of Princeton University Press.

All biblical quotations are taken from the New Revised Standard Version Bible, copyright © 1989, Division of Christian Education of the National Council of the Churches of Christ in the U. S. A., and used by permission. All rights reserved.

"If only it were all so simple! If only there were evil people somewhere insidiously committing evil deeds, and it were necessary only to separate them from the rest of us and destroy them. But the line dividing good and evil cuts through the heart of every human being. And who is willing to destroy a piece of his own heart?"

—Aleksandr Solzhenitsyn, *The Gulag Archipelago*

Contents

Preface / ix

1. Pursuing Eternity / 1
2. Barriers to Willing One Thing / 18
3. The Price of Willing One Thing / 45
4. What Then Must I Do? / 55
5. Kierkegaardian Faith / 71

   Epilogue / 94

   Index / 95

Preface

THE MASTER analysts of the human psyche have all probed inner dividedness. Though they have depicted this dividedness in different ways, they all agree that it is central to understanding who we are. They have also agreed that we desperately want to be rid of it. We crave to be unified within and free from inner dissension.

Soren Kierkegaard's *Purity of Heart Is to Will One Thing* is a master analysis of our inner dividedness. In this striking little book, Kierkegaard gently yet incisively describes the precise forms dividedness takes. His discerning and all-too-accurate descriptions of it unveil the real motives that drive us.

The kind of dividedness Kierkegaard explores in *Purity of Heart* is that between a single-minded commitment to goodness and the numerous wayward motives that undermine this commitment. We want, to use Anne Morrow Lindbergh's words, "a singleness of eye, a purity of intention, a central core," but find, as C. S. Lewis so graphically put it, that we are "a zoo of lusts, a bedlam of ambitions, a nursery of fears, a harem of fondled hatreds."[1] We genuinely desire what is good but find ourselves swayed by numerous enticements that undermine the desire.

---

1. Anne Morrow Lindbergh, *Gift from the Sea* (New York: Pantheon Books, 1975), 17; C. S. Lewis, *Surprised by Joy: The Shape of My Early Life* (San Diego: Harvest Books, 1955), 226.

Like many of Soren Kierkegaard's books, however, *Purity of Heart* contains a good deal of formidable prose. To be sure, numerous passages are wonderfully and clearly written, beautiful even in their flowing and lyrical style. But many other passages are opaque and seem disconnected from the main theme. My aim is to make Kierkegaard's exploration of our inner terrain accessible and inviting.

The Divided Soul follows the format of *Purity of Heart*. I start with introductory matters—eternity's emissaries, the hidden self, and what it means to will the good single-mindedly. I then work through Kierkegaard's descriptions of the barriers to purity of heart, the various ways, that is, in which we are divided. Next I deal with the requirements for willing one thing, that is, the price—commitment and the exposure of evasions. "What Then Must I Do?" goes into what Kierkegaard means by living as an individual, which he regards as the remedy for dividedness. And in the last chapter I reflect on some of the main themes in the book, balancing them with a larger perspective.

The translation I quote from is by Howard V. Hong and Edna H. Hong, published by Princeton University Press in 1993 as part of Volume 15 of *Kierkegaard's Writings*. Page numbers in the text are to this translation. *Purity of Heart* was originally titled "An Occasional Discourse" and appeared in 1847 as the first section of a larger book called *Upbuilding Discourses in Various Spirits*. It has come to be known as *Purity of Heart Is to Will One Thing* because Kierkegaard wrote early in it, "So let us on the occasion of a confession speak on this theme: Purity of Heart Is to Will One Thing" (24).

Thanks go to Daniel Crow, who read the manuscript twice and gave me numerous insightful suggestions, and to my wife, Linda Williams, who also made numerous insightful suggestions. I also have benefited from an earlier translation of *Purity of Heart* by Douglas Steere, published in 1948 by Harper and Brothers.

I remind the reader, as did Kierkegaard, that the author is an everyday sort of person who knows too well his own dividedness. This book is as much confession as it is exploration of the inner life.

1

Pursuing Eternity

TO EVERYTHING THERE IS A SEASON— EXCEPT THE PURSUIT OF ETERNITY

KIERKEGAARD BEGINS *Purity of Heart* by contrasting seasons for dancing with seasons for remembering. There is a time to dance and a time to sit still, a time to live for the future and a time to live in one's memories. Youth in its vigor dances and twirls with delight. The aged sit quietly, moving only now and then, slowly and with little vigor. Youth excitedly looks toward the day of marriage, job, adventure, and change. Age simply remembers good times and bad.

Even a flower, if it could speak, would describe its seasons: "there is a time to play lightheartedly with the spring breezes and a time to be snapped off by the autumn storms . . . a time to be sought out for its loveliness and a time to be unrecognizable in its wretchedness" (10). An animal, too, would know that "there is a time to leap for joy and a time to crawl along the ground . . . a time to run with the herd and a time to go apart to die" (10).

To everything there is a season, Solomon says, but Kierkegaard reminds us that Solomon also says that God has put a sense of eternity into human hearts (Ecclesiastes 3:11).

This sense does not age or grow dim. It is always present. We cannot say, "I will dance while I am young and think about eternity when I am older." The eternal in us is the one thing that transcends all seasons.

Suppose, says Kierkegaard, we were to think of eternity as having its own time. We would then say to ourselves, "there is a time to be carefree and a time to be crushed in repentance" (13). If we thought in this way, there would be danger, "a danger that is called going astray" (13). We would think that we could put off the pursuit of eternity and take it up another time. Perhaps we would. It is more likely that we would not. Delay leads to more delay, which solidifies the original procrastination. This procrastination continues and controls us until we have forgotten the eternal altogether.

THE ELEVENTH HOUR

There is, consequently, a sense of urgency about pursuing eternity. Kierkegaard uses the idea of being at "the eleventh hour" to describe this sense. To be at the eleventh hour is to be near the last moment, when we experience a "concern of inwardness" that is sharpened by regret (14). It is to be close to midnight with little time left, or almost at death when soon all will be over.

What we need to do, Kierkegaard says, is to think of the call to seek eternity as coming at the eleventh hour. If we do not, we will postpone responding to it. That, in fact, is what we do. Those who are young think there is plenty of time for examining their motives. Those who are old think the same; to them death is still a long way off. For both, it is not "Tomorrow I will begin to assess my life" but "I have many years left."

We understand life differently when we think of God's call as coming always at the eleventh hour, Kierkegaard suggests. If we were to picture ourselves as being 79, without deluding ourselves about how many more years we have, we would ask ourselves questions we customarily avoid. We would wonder whether we had frittered away our time in trivialities. We would reflect on whether we had avoided real love, whether we had used our energy just to get ahead, and whether we had run from God whenever God got close. We would not want to be consumed with regret.

ETERNITY'S EMISSARIES

The call of eternity, then, comes at the eleventh hour. But how does it come? Kierkegaard focuses on two "messengers": regret and repentance. There are, of course, others, which I shall say something about later. For now we can note that he deals with just these two because the aim of *Purity of Heart* is to describe the proper preparation for confession, both as a "holy act" on a Sunday morning and as a "quiet daily concern" (19). More importantly, he focuses on regret and repentance because they are necessary for single-minded pursuit of the eternal. Delay obstructs that pursuit, but regret and repentance lead us to the good.

"So strange a power is regret, so sincere is its friendship, that there is in fact nothing more terrible than to have escaped it entirely" (13). The essence of regret is sorrowing and grieving for sins. Repentance adds a movement away from the object of sorrow and grief, and together they awaken an active desire for the good. It can be put more strongly: they change our hearts. We no longer are indifferent to the eternal.

"Busyness and proud striving and impatient passion" (16) cease to control us. Wanting to get ahead does not dominate us. We make efforts to break free from our addictions. The thing we come to fear most is to live as if dead. Indeed, life would be a living death if we had no regret or repentance.

ILLUSORY REPENTANCE

One significant way not to be repentant is mistakenly to think we are. In this case we wrongly think we are repenting because we identify repentance with other more common inner states. Kierkegaard describes two such states. One is impatient grieving and the other is striving to become better.

Suppose we were to have a sudden sense of what we took to be grief for sin. Suppose also that we wanted immediately to push it aside. In this case, we would be impatient to get beyond the grief; we would be in a hurry to do or think something else. The grief would not be an honest repentance, for it would really be impatience that moves us.

Or suppose that we gave up certain undesirable ways of acting and adopted new ways but did not possess either sorrow for our old ways or a desire that the new ones exemplify goodness. We gave up a destructive habit, for example, or got into a volunteer organization and engaged in worthy conduct but had no grief for the past or passion for the good. In this case, too, there would be no real repentance, though we may have thought so, for there would be no "silent daily concern" (18).

What we lack in both of these cases is an "inwardness" that regrets "the guilt more and more fervently" (18). We also lack a desire for "progress in the good" (19). Impatient grieving lacks these because with it we desire nothing more than a short, intense experience. Mere improvement in observable character also lacks these because with it we want only a change of externals—not in addition a quiet, searching passion. Neither would embrace the change of heart required for pursuing the eternal.

THE HIDDEN SELF

The possibility of illusory repentance suggests that some of what goes on inside us is hidden from us. Perhaps it would be more accurate to say that some of our internal states are half-hidden. For, as Kierkegaard so aptly puts it, we both see them and do not see them (20). It is as if, he says, we observe them through half-closed eyes.

Consider an analogy. Our visual field has a central part and a peripheral part. In the central part we see what is straight in front of us with clarity and distinctness. In the larger, peripheral part, there are gradations of awareness. In the outermost regions we have only a dim awareness, but our awareness becomes less dim as it approaches the center. Our attention is naturally focused on the central part, and we must make an effort to discover what is in the peripheral part. If something moves in the peripheral part, we must look directly at it in order to see it clearly. Most of our field of vision is in the peripheral part.

Our moral selves are like our field of vision. We have commitments and aims of which, some of the time, we are fully conscious. We also have motives and desires of which we are less conscious. Two examples that Kierkegaard mentions are "pride that mixes in even with sympathy, and envy that mixes in even with friendship" (23). We certainly may be fully conscious of these, and, indeed, are at times. When we are, we feel a bit of shame, perhaps inadequacy as well, maybe even bitter regret if the sympathy and friendship are important to us. More often, though, we are less aware of them. It feels in fact as if we are not aware of them at all much of the time. Like the objects at the farthest edges of our peripheral vision, we must take active steps to get them into sharper focus.

In saying that we see yet do not see pride and envy, Kierkegaard accounts both for our accessibility to them and for their hiddenness. If someone were to say that we see pride and envy clearly and distinctly, that would not be true to the facts. The fact is that pride and envy are often rather hazy. But if they were said to be totally eclipsed and never ascertainable, that too would not be true to the facts. We can become aware of them and do so on occasion, usually painfully. We see them much more clearly than we would like. So it is true both that we see and do not see the motives in the outer regions of our moral selves.

There is, however, an important difference between the half-seen parts of our field of vision and the obscure segments of our moral selves. It is that the half-seen parts of our vision are a result of simple ignorance, whereas the obscure knowledge of our moral selves is a result of deliberate resistance to the good. We do not want to know about pride and envy. So we move them out of full awareness to the region of half-awareness.

Kierkegaard says of simple ignorance that it can be remedied simply by learning more. He calls deliberate ignorance "self-deception" (23), which means that it is a willed ignorance. Simply learning more will not remedy it; we must also have a change of will. In *Sickness unto Death* Kierkegaard refers to the first kind of ignorance as an "original ignorance" and to the second as a "resultant, a later ignorance."[1] An original ignorance is not produced by a person's efforts; it exists naturally, as does the peripheral part of our vision. We just haven't looked in the right place. A resultant ignorance, however, "must lodge in a person's efforts to obscure his knowing."[2] We see pride and envy clearly, do not like them, and so push them into obscurity. It is not just that we do not see them.

We also will to be ignorant of our desire to be virtuous. The same part of us that does not want to know about pride and envy also does not want to know about our desire for the good. If we saw this desire clearly, we would also see pride and envy clearly. So in resisting goodness we push both pride and desire for the good into obscurity.

This resultant ignorance is produced by what Kierkegaard calls a "dialectic," or interplay, between knowing and willing. Knowing comes first—we glimpse pride or we sense that we have engaged in incriminating gossip. Willing comes next—we do not want to continue gazing at the pride and are unwilling to stay aware of the gossip. Ignorance comes last—we no longer are fully aware of the pride, and gossip does not seem quite so bad. Of course, it is not so simple as this. The process is gradual and we constantly go back and forth between the stages. We might say to ourselves, "I will think about this tomorrow," and as tomorrow comes, the clarity of our knowing

---

1. Soren Kierkegaard, *The Sickness unto Death: A Christian Psychological Exposition for Upbuilding and Awakening*, edited and translated by Howard V. Hong and Edna H. Hong (Princeton, NJ: Princeton University Press, 1980), 88.

2. Ibid., 88.

decreases. With this decrease comes a decrease in the force of willing. And this leads to further ignorance.

An interplay between knowing and willing also occurs when we seek to uncover hidden motives. However, the willing is different from what it is when we obscure our motives. Instead of resistance to goodness, we will the good. This willing makes us want to know the desires we have relegated to obscurity. It moves us to discover the tactics we use to resist the good. When, for example, we become aware of the difference between wanting to do well and wanting to be better than others, we may perceive that it is really the latter and not the former that has motivated us. Or when we come to know how ulterior motives operate, we may recognize that it is they that have driven us instead of a desire for goodness.

We can see now how the shifting between half-hidden awareness of our inner lives and full awareness is like the shifting that takes place between the peripheral and central parts of our visual fields. There is another similarity between our moral selves and our peripheral vision. I said earlier that most of our visual field consists of the peripheral part. Something similar seems to be true of our moral selves. We are fully conscious of only a small portion of our "moral sight"—what we are aware of about our moral motives, good and bad, right and wrong. The rest we hide. We "work gradually at eclipsing [our] ethical and ethical-religious comprehension," Kierkegaard states.[3] Dostoevsky's underground man makes a similar observation about our darker regions: "There are certain things in a man's past which he does not divulge to everybody but, perhaps, only to his friends. Again there are certain things he will not divulge even to his friends; he will divulge them

3. Ibid., 94.

perhaps only to himself, and that, too, as a secret. But, finally, there are things which he is afraid to divulge even to himself, and every decent man has quite an accumulation of such things in his mind. I can put it even this way: the more decent a man is, the larger will the number of such things be."[4] If this is true, then we are largely strangers to ourselves—by choice. Most of who we are, morally and religiously, is unknown to us—by design. This is a rather unsettling truth, for we like to think that we have done nothing to obstruct knowledge of ourselves and that we know ourselves fairly well.

What happens, then, when we resist the good is that our self-knowledge is constricted. We know neither our virtuous nor our questionable motives. When we will the good, however, our self-knowledge is enlarged. We come to know segments of our moral selves that hitherto we did not suspect existed.

WILLING ONE THING

Willing the good, then, is needed in order to know the half-hidden parts of our moral selves. But what is it to will the good? The essence of the idea is easy to grasp—we will the good and only the good. We do not resist it, we do not will it for ulterior reasons, and we do not possess other motives that obscure it. In Kierkegaard's words, we "divest [ourselves] of multiplicity in order to make up [our] mind about one thing" (19).

---

4. Fyodor Dostoevsky, "Notes from the Underground," *The Best Short Stories of Dostoevsky*, trans. David Magarshack (New York: The Modern Library, n.d.), 144.

To unpack this idea, I shall explain Kierkegaard's claim that we can will only the good single-mindedly and then what it is to have two wills.

Only the Good Can Be Willed Single-mindedly

This is a surprising claim. Why cannot we will anything else single-mindedly? The answer Kierkegaard gives is that only the good is one thing. All else contains "manyness." Consider some examples: pleasure, honor, wealth, and power (26). One might think that we could desire these single-mindedly, pursuing them with a pure, though misguided, passion. In reality, the pursuit of each involves multiplicity and change. With pleasure, we get one gratification after another. We are not content with just one kind of pleasure, but continually want new ones. The same is true of the pursuit of honor. We must have new people who admire us. Perhaps we flatter our enemies or court the favor of those whom we despise (28). We might even betray acquaintances we esteem in order to obtain praise (28). It is no different with wealth and power. For these we have a "restless preoccupation" and a desire for continually increasing amounts (28). Having more breeds the desire for still more.

Moreover, none of these lasts. Each is changed into something else when it becomes too intense. Extreme pleasure turns into a kind of disgust. Enjoying honor becomes contempt for others. Relishing one's riches changes into discontent. The feeling of power becomes the feeling of dependence for our power on those over whom we have power, which amounts to slavery. And each is lost at death. The pleasures, honors, riches, and power we pursue die when we die.

In eternity we will no longer have any of these, nor will we be able to obtain more.

Consider another example: momentary enthusiasm. This, too, might appear to be the sort of state in which we could be willing one thing, even if for only a short time. Kierkegaard responds as before: it doesn't last. The passionate resolution, the exhilarating hope, the sharp regret all fade and are forgotten. In order to be willing one thing, we must will it continually. It cannot be an on-and-off phenomenon. That is not truly willing *one* thing.

What about an enthusiasm that does remain? Would not this be an example of single-minded devotion? Here Kierkegaard concedes a bit. If we were to sacrifice our own concerns for a cause, constantly pursuing it, and living and dying for it, we may indeed be willing one thing (35). We would have to be careful, though, for our willing could take a wrong turn. Still, our single-minded enthusiasm would aid us in coming to will the good single-mindedly, for we would see what it would be like to will something singly.

In looking at these examples, we learn that what Kierkegaard means by willing the good single-mindedly is that there is a unity in our willing—we do not will part here and part there, or part now and part later, as we do for pleasure and honor. He also means that there is a constancy in our willing—we do not change from week to week or from this life to the next. In true loving, for example, the one who loves "does not love once for all; neither does he use a portion of his love now and then in turn another portion.... No, he loves with all his love; it is totally present in every expression; he continually spends all of it, and yet he continually keeps it all in his heart. What marvelous wealth!" (30), Kierkegaard exclaims.

Two Wills

We can discover more about willing the good single-mindedly by looking at what it is to have "two wills." What happens here is that our willing goes in opposite directions. We both desire the good and resist it. In this simple observation, Kierkegaard has pointed to what may be the most significant fact about human nature. Ernest Becker, in discussing Kierkegaard, calls it "the basic insight of psychology for all time," which is, in his words, that people are "a union of opposites."[5] The novelist Zora Neale Hurston describes the fact picturesquely: "Everybody is two beings: one lives and flourishes in the daylight and stands guard. The other being walks and howls at night."[6]

One form this opposition takes is conscious struggle. Here we are fully aware both of our desire for the good and of our resistance to it. This duality Kierkegaard calls an "anguished double-mindedness" (33), because we want both sides of the opposition and yet do not want the opposition. We genuinely want the good—our doing so is not an illusion—but we also genuinely do not want it. And we do not like being split in this way. So our desire for the good is agonizing, because our resistance to it keeps us from having it simply and purely. And we know this. The night howler in us knows about our

---

5. Ernest Becker, *The Denial of Death* (New York: The Free Press, 1973), 68. Becker doesn't quite get the opposites right, calling them "self-consciousness" and "physical body" (68–69). The context is an explanation of Kierkegaard's view of human nature, which arises from the doctrine of the Fall.

6. Zora Neale Hurston, *Moses, Man of the Mountain* (New York: HarperPerennial, 1991), 60.

daylight flourishing, and our daylight persona knows that at night it will howl. And both despair over the duality.

Augustine experienced this dividedness sharply as he neared the moment he surrendered himself to God. On the one hand, he felt bound to his old habits. These habits, originating with his own choices, had become necessity and were restraining him from changing. On the other hand, though his desire to serve God was becoming stronger, it was not strong enough to enable him to break free from them. "So," he writes, "my two wills, one old, the other new, one carnal, the other spiritual, were in conflict with one another." It is not, he continues, that these two wills form two rival substances in him. There is but one self: "the self which willed to serve was identical with the self which was unwilling. It was I. I was neither wholly willing nor wholly unwilling."[7]

Kierkegaard mirrors these last words: "Just as a person, despite all his defiance, does not have the power to tear himself away completely from the good, because it is the stronger, he also does not even have the power to will it completely" (33). We want to be free from our continual resistance to the good (because we do indeed desire the good), but find that we cannot, because our resistance is so persistent. So we are caught between two opposing desires, both real and both tenacious.

Consider loving generously. In an honest moment, we would reveal that this is what we want our lives to be about, what at 79 we would like to look back on with a well-placed contentment. But in the same honest moment, we would admit that we do not much want to be generous in our loving

---

7. Augustine, *Confessions*, trans. Henry Chadwick (Oxford: Oxford University Press, 1991), Book VIII, secs. 5 and 10, 140, 148.

or even to be loving. The power each want has over us lessens the power of the other, so that we neither wholly want to love nor wholly want not to.

Conscious struggle is not the only way in which we possess two wills. There is too much we hide for this to be so. Augustinian anguish is more commonly muted, and the opposition between desiring and resisting the good is more often submerged into half-consciousness. Consider humility and pride.

We might, first, have a clearly conscious desire for humility pitted against a half-conscious desire for pride. This is as much a case of willing two things as when we are fully conscious of both desires. An obscured desire does not disappear just because we do not observe it clearly. And it controls us as much as, perhaps more than, a conscious desire. The same is true when we are clearly conscious of a desire for pride but obscurely aware of a desire for humility. In this situation, the resistance to goodness in us blinds us to our desire for humility, but it still exists, and moves us. The case is no different when both our desire for pride and our desire for humility are half-conscious. In this circumstance, our two wills would be even more hidden. They would, nevertheless, be there, moving us in ways which we are not aware of. In each of these half-conscious situations, to use Zora Neale Hurston's words, we are only vaguely aware of the split between our daytime guard and nighttime howler. Yet we guard and howl all the same.

Having half-hidden ulterior motives also illustrates inner opposition. An example that Kierkegaard mentions in *Practice in Christianity* is inquiring into the feelings of one who is suffering. Our ostensible aim in doing this is to exhibit sympathy, but our hidden aim is to satisfy curiosity. "Ah, human sympathy," he writes, "how often was it only curiosity, not sympathy, that made you dare to venture into a sufferer's secret."[8] We might, of course, be aware of the curiosity and inquire anyway (the resistance to goodness in us brazenly drives us on). But it is more likely that we have submerged the curiosity (again, out of resistance and just as brazenly).

This is a case of willing oppositely, because we retain the desire to act sympathetically without an ulterior motive even though we also want, unknown to us, to act sympathetically for the sake of curiosity. Put differently, we want to give unalloyed sympathy, while at the same time we resist this good by mixing curiosity with it. Illusory sympathy both attracts and repels us.

The aim in all this should be to raise both our half-hidden resistance to the good and our submerged desire for the good into full consciousness. When our resistance acts on us half-hiddenly, it controls us. And when our desire for the good is submerged, it doesn't control us enough.

Willing the good single-mindedly, we now see, is to will the good without resisting it and without having ulterior motives. It is to will the good and only the good—humility and only humility, sympathy and only sympathy. When we do this, we flourish in the daylight and do not howl at night.

---

8. Soren Kierkegaard, *Practice in Christianity*, edited and translated by Howard V. Hong and Edna H. Hong (Princeton, NJ: Princeton University Press, 1991), 21.

THE GOOD AND THE ETERNAL

I have been using "the good" and "the eternal" without explanation. Kierkegaard does so as well. Nowhere in *Purity of Heart* does he tell us what he means by these. He seems to have assumed that we will know what he is referring to. This, it seems to me, is a reasonable assumption, given two features of his audience. The first is that the people to whom Kierkegaard was writing were everyday people, not scholars, theologians, or philosophers. As such, they would have had intuitive ideas about what the good and the eternal are, and would not have asked abstruse questions about them. In addition, his audience consisted of people who regarded both themselves and Kierkegaard as Christians. They would, therefore, naturally have interpreted these phrases in Christian ways. Here is how I think we should understood them.

The good is simply "what is good." Willing the good single-mindedly, then, is willing love or kindness single-mindedly. To add a Christian dimension to this would be to include Christian virtues and activities in what is good, such as humility and gratitude to God, confession of sin and encouragement of other believers. Willing the good then becomes willing all of these single-mindedly.

The eternal is a combination of two ideas. It is what is most important about life—what we believe really counts—and it is life beyond death with God. These two ideas are connected in the Christian scheme of things. It is only what really counts that will last beyond death. And life after death with God consists only of what counts. In referring to the eternal, Kierkegaard sometimes has mainly the first idea in mind, and at other times he has the second in mind as well. At times he contrasts the eternal with unimportant pursuits—honor and riches, for example—and at other times he refers to the next life, as when he says that in eternity God will judge us for our double-mindedness or give us a "crown of honor" for having willed only one thing (29). I have followed Kierkegaard's practice.

With these clarifications, we can see that the pursuit of the good and the pursuit of the eternal are the same. That is why Kierkegaard calls purity of heart the "one thing needful" (24). If we do not have it, we do not have the one thing that really counts in life or the one thing that will carry us into eternity. We will be victims of the most terrible delusion of all—thinking that we love God and are open to God's grace when in fact we are driven by other motives.

2

Barriers to Willing One Thing

REWARD

For Love of Her Money

IMAGINE A man loving a woman only for her money. He does all the things lovers normally do. He talks to her with respect and gentleness. He displays affection, gives her gifts on her birthday, and is attentive when she talks to him. But, Kierkegaard asks rhetorically, "Who would call him a lover?" (38). We would not even say that he loves her for her money, because he does not love her at all. He loves only her money. Nor would we say that he gets the money as a reward for loving her, for he cannot get a reward for what does not exist.

Two features of this case are readily apparent. The first is that love for the woman is distinct from love for her money. Each can be present without the other. Only love for the woman's money is present in this case, though it might have been that only love for the woman was present. The second is that the appearance of love for the woman differs from real love for her. The man only appears to love her; he does not really do so. Again, it could have been different—his appearance of love might have reflected real love.

Now let us suppose that the man tells us that he really does love her and not her money. How should we respond? We might say (if we could be candid), "It is difficult to tell. Money is alluring, and it might be attracting you even though you say it is not. We cannot suppose you really love her just because you say you do. In fact, you cannot be so sure either. What you have to do is test yourself—wish that she did not have the money, or ask her to give it away. Then see how you feel."

The woman herself might think she is loved, even though she is not. The appearance of love in the man fits her conception of what love is. She likes his attention and kindness. So it is possible for her to be deceived also. And if, in fact, her money is very important to her, she too may be presenting to the man only the appearance of love, for what she may really want is to be admired for her wealth. She would love the man only for his admiration, which is to say that she would not love him at all.

The situation is the same for loving the good. If we love the good only for what we get from doing so, we are not really loving the good. "The good is one thing; the reward is something else," Kierkegaard states (37). And he goes on to say that if we love the good for the sake of the reward, we are not actually loving it. It only appears as if we do. In order actually to love the good, we must love it "without regard for reward" (39).

The Lure of Reward

None of this would matter much if the reward were not enticing. We might say with a flip of the hand, "I am not tempted into false love." We might hold up the Sophists, say, as examples of wanting the good for the sake of reward. All they wanted, we would observe, is for people to think they were wise so that they could be paid for teaching their brand of wisdom. But none of us is tempted any longer to do that, we would declare. People would see through it instantly.

Things are not so easy, however. The rewards are enticing. Consider admiration. We might truly say, "I am not doing this for the money," but who can say, "I never do anything in order to be admired"? The truth is that we can scarcely live if we do not have a generous dose of admiration. We rarely pass through a conscious hour without the memory or hope of praise. "It is a common human craving to be looked upon as someone great," Kierkegaard states in *For Self-Examination*. Then he adds, "and the common fakery is to pass oneself off for something more than one is."[1]

The temptation to appear good is intensified when we are offered opportunities to feel admired, which we constantly are. Public recognition, small and large, is given in numerous ways. Commendation comes from work associates. Friends compliment us. If we are in a position of authority, we obtain deference from those subordinate to us. When our virtue is noticed, as it almost always is, it receives favorable attention. Some of us become local heroes. And all of these occasions for feeling admired exist in religious contexts just as much as they do in secular ones.

We are lured, therefore, almost irresistibly to appear good. This is not too strong a way to put it, for, as Kierkegaard

---

1. Soren Kierkegaard, *For Self-Examination* and *Judge for Yourself!* edited and translated by Howard V. Hong and Edna H. Hong (Princeton, NJ: Princeton University Press, 1990), 59.

noted, we possess a burning desire to be thought great. So it is a dodge to dismiss the possibility of false love because we think we will never love for money. We are not too likely to do this, to be sure, but we are almost certain to want to act virtuously for the admiration it confers.

Kierkegaard describes a couple of cases in which we succumb to the lure. In the first, though we begin by being genuinely virtuous, we gradually become weary. Perhaps there is too much opposition to the good we do and too little gratitude. We picture ourselves being admired and we wonder whether one can be both virtuous and admired. It is not the admiration that is at fault, we reason—rightly, no doubt—for we have no control over other people's attitudes toward us. We can in fact accept their admiration and still be genuinely virtuous, we conclude. Soon, however, we are acting in virtuous ways in order to get the admiration.

In the second case, we again begin with genuine virtue. But we notice—we are not naive—that other seemingly virtuous people are admired. We ask ourselves why we cannot be like them. "Why must we be alone in this?" we agonize. So we give in. We "give up the good" (44) and go after the admiration, though of course still appearing to love the good.

What Are We Really After?

Kierkegaard gives us two tests that we can use to discover whether we are willing the good or willing the reward. The first is to ask whether we are anxious about the ill effects of willing the good. "Good is often rewarded temporarily with ingratitude, with lack of appreciation, with poverty, with contempt, with many sufferings, at times with death" (39). If we are worried about these occurring because of our good, it is likely that we want the good only because of what we get for it—gratitude, appreciation, perhaps even a bit of honor. But if we will the good without being anxious about whether we will get gratitude or appreciation, we will it single-mindedly. That is, we will the good and only the good.

The second test is to imagine that the reward is absent. Would we still will the good? Consider someone who visits a nursing home to talk to the residents. She searches the faces of those to whom she talks to see how she stands with them, to see whether she is given proper regard. If she does not get it, she wants to leave. She talks to the residents merely to acquire their regard. That is what moves her and not love of the good.

Kierkegaard is not saying that it would be better not to get any rewards. Some rewards, in fact, are good to get—gratitude, for instance. Gratitude is good both in the giving and in the receiving. This is true, too, of appreciation. Why should we not graciously accept the appreciation of others for our goodness? Praise and admiration can also be accepted in the same way. They are, in fact, necessary for the formation of a healthy self-concept in maturing children. What Kierkegaard is saying is that we should not think of gratitude, appreciation, praise, and admiration as rewards for our goodness. For we would then be wanting to be good in order to get them.

Kierkegaard takes the same stance toward the reward God will give us after we die. It is as certain as anything can be, he declares, that God in eternity will add more goodness to the good we have done before we enter eternity. And it is entirely appropriate to want what God will give us then. But, again, we should not want it as a reward. On this matter, there is no difference between pre-death reward and post-death reward: we are not willing the good if all we want the good for is to obtain the reward. Kierkegaard does not think, however, that willing the good only to get God's reward is nearly as much of a temptation as is willing the good only to get the world's rewards—admiration, honor, and gratitude from significant people. These we can scarcely resist.

FEAR OF PUNISHMENT

For Fear of Her Disapproval

Now imagine a man loving a woman because he fears her disapproval. Something deep in his psyche moves him to seek the approval of women, perhaps because he did not have maternal love as a child. He desperately needs female love and just as desperately fears female disapproval. He finds a woman whom he thinks he loves and he gives her attention and affection. Though it appears as if he loves her, in reality he merely wants her approval and fears her disapproval. If the man were to tell us that his love was genuine, we might reply, "Our real motives for what we do are often submerged. If you know that your childhood privation is not illegitimately affecting you, then you can know that you are loving for real. Otherwise you are probably just acting out your need for female approval."

The woman might think she is genuinely loved, for she does not see what really drives the man. And her love for him might be motivated only by a need to be feared. If so, she would also be presenting only the appearance of love. Neither of them would actually love each other. If we did not know about their submerged drives, we might exclaim, "How wonderfully they love each other!"

Fear-driven Goodness

Our fear of "punishment" is as strong as our attraction to reward. The main form of this "punishment" is disapproval. We fear it as much as we want admiration. From early infancy onward we shrink in dejection when someone expresses disapproval toward us. It does not matter whether that person is someone we know or a stranger we meet and never see again. Our whole day would be ruined if a passing pedestrian stopped in front of us and declared, "You're pretty ugly." More than a day would be ruined if we were constantly criticized by a parent.

To prevent disapproval, we change. Perhaps we put on makeup, wear different clothes, or redo our hair. We refrain from the behavior that brought parental disapproval. If we are with people who hold intelligence in high regard, we act more intelligently. If it is social propriety that they esteem, we make certain our mannerisms are proper. And—here we come to the point—if it is goodness that our associates value, we put on a display of goodness.

The fear-driven person is one who is a slave to others' disapproval. She is continually intent on knowing what they think of her. Her aim is to ward off shame from their judgment, or from what she takes to be their judgment. Her goodness is like makeup. She is anxious about how it looks and worries that something has gone wrong with it. She constantly checks it to ensure its presentability. An impartial observer would say that her life is both false and unhappy.

Good-driven Fear

When Kierkegaard says that "someone who wills the good only out of fear of punishment does not will the good in truth" (52), he has in mind two kinds of punishment. The first is what he calls earthly and temporal punishment. The examples he gives of this are "financial loss, loss of reputation, lack of appreciation, disregard, the opinion of the world, the mockery of fools, the laughter of light-mindedness, the cowardly whining of deference, the inflated insignificance of the moment, the delusive, misty apparitions of miasma" (52). Several of these are rather opaque, but that need not prevent us from seeing what he is after. To will the good out of fear of earthly punishment, he is saying, is to will it to avoid such undesirable conditions as ridicule and loss of prestige.

The second kind of punishment is divine punishment in eternity. About this Kierkegaard says that we do not fear it nearly so much as we do the first kind of punishment. What he appears to mean by this is that we fear human disapproval and loss of prestige more, because they are more immediate and strike at our intense desire to be admired. It is much more of a temptation, therefore, to will the good in order to avoid earthly punishment than it is to will the good to avoid divine punishment. If we thought about the matter, of course, we would have more fear of divine punishment. But we usually do not think of it, wanting only to prevent others' disapproval. In spite of this difference between the two kinds of punishment, they are alike in that to will the good out of fearing either is not to will the good at all. "The good is one thing, punishment something else" (44)—no matter what kind of punishment it is.

Having said this, however, Kierkegaard tells us that there is a legitimate way of fearing divine punishment. In this way we think of divine punishment as the right consequence for doing wrong. We do not fear it simply because we dislike it, as we do human disapproval and loss of prestige. We fear it as part of our aversion to doing wrong, because the punishment is required by the wrong. Nor do we wish it were absent in the same way we wish human disapproval and loss of prestige were absent. We wish it absent because we wish not to do wrong. We say, "I do not want to do what would deserve divine punishment—not because it will be punished but because it is wrong." Of human disapproval, however, we say, "I do not like it. If it were not for it, I would not display goodness"—thereby demonstrating that it is not the goodness we want but the approval and prestige. But it is both the divine punishment and the wrong that we are averse to if we fear divine punishment in the right way.

The right shame, therefore, is to be shamed before the good, that is, to feel shame when we do not do what is good. The wrong shame comes when we feel it simply because of how others would react to us if we did not do what is good. Put differently and a bit obliquely, we have the right shame when we are alone, and the wrong shame when we are with others. The one shame produces "being"; the other "seeming." What Kierkegaard means by this is that the right shame leads us really to be good, whereas the wrong shame leads us only to appear good. "What is it to be more ashamed before others than before oneself but to be more ashamed of seeming than of being?" (53).

What we need is to have the right fear without also having the wrong fear. If we do not have the right fear, it is because of "defiance and obstinacy and self-willfulness" (46). We are willfully not doing the good and willfully not fearing the wrong. If we have the wrong fear, it is because of "cravenness and servility and hypocrisy" (46). We are afraid that other people will disapprove of us if we do not do what is good. The "good" that we do is driven only by fear. The right fear, however, is motivated by a desire to possess the good and to avoid the wrong. It is good-driven.

An example of these two kinds of fear is contained in Daniel Defoe's *Moll Flanders*. After thirty years of prostitution, bigamy, and thievery, Moll is caught stealing and sent to Newgate Prison. There, knowing that thieves are commonly hanged, she repents, first falsely and then genuinely. She writes, "Then I repented heartily of all my life past, but that repentance yielded me no satisfaction, no peace, no, not in the least, because, as I said to myself, it was repenting after the power of farther sinning was taken away. I seemed not to mourn that I had committed such crimes, and for the fact as it was an offence against God and my neighbor, but that I was to be punished for it. I was a penitent, as I thought, not that I had sinned, but that I was to suffer."[2] Her false repentance is fear-driven: "all my repentance appeared to me to be only the effect of my fear of death, not a sincere regret for the wicked life that I had lived."[3] Later, however, she repents genuinely: "I was covered with shame and tears for things past, and yet had at the same time a secret, surprising joy at the prospect of being a true penitent."[4]

2. Daniel Defoe, *Moll Flanders* (New York: Dutton Signet, 1996), 242–43.

3. Ibid., 245.

4. Ibid., 255.

An instance of good-driven fear is the motivation Eve and Adam had before they were tempted to eat the apple. What they wanted instinctively and naturally, because God had implanted the desire in them, was to be good. They also must have wanted the good consequences of their goodness. God no doubt had promised these consequences to them if they were good, not as a prize, but as a natural outgrowth of their goodness, just as God had threatened them with punishment if they ate the apple. They did not act well just to get the good consequences or to avoid the punishment. If they had, they would not really have been acting well. Instead, their motivation was a pure desire to be good and an earnest fear of doing wrong.

EGOCENTRIC SERVICE OF THE GOOD

"I Do the Good"

Abraham Heschel asks, "Who can be sure whether he is worshipping his own ego ... while ostensibly adoring God?"[5] This is the kind of question Kierkegaard would like. Self-admiration, he asserts, is as much a craving as the craving to be thought great. We are motivated to do the good by the one as much as by the other.

Consider a person who gives sandwiches to the homeless on the streets of Chicago. She gathers friends to go with her. They walk along Broadway, stop at a drop-in center, and talk to the street people they meet. Later she says, "I will go alone so as not to be admired." She does—and tells no one.

---

5. Abraham Joshua Heschel, *A Passion for Truth* (New York: Farrar, Straus and Giroux, 1973), 95.

She banishes the thought that her friends would admire her if they knew. She even sets aside the desire that the people she talks to admire her. Wonderful humility! But, alas, there is one thing left. She says to herself, "*I* am doing this good thing." No one else may notice the good she does, but she does. And it is this which prompts her solitary sandwiching.

Kierkegaard's way of putting this point is to say that willing the good is one thing and willing its victory through us is another (61). What he means is that there is a difference between our wanting to do *good* and *our* wanting to do good. In the former we have no thought that we are the one by whom the good comes, whereas in the latter it is this thought that motivates us. We picture ourselves being the instrument, almost the chosen one, through whom the homeless will be fed. We do not understand that this good can come without us. Indeed, we choose not to understand this, because we are wed to self-admiration.

Impatience often hides this ulterior motive. We hurl ourselves into a work of compassion, wanting to hasten its victory, that is, wanting to make sure that it succeeds rapidly and well. We press ourselves into service, becoming busy for the sake of those who suffer. To be sure, we do not do so to get gratitude from the recipients of our compassion or to get admiration from our associates. But we are moved by a sense of pride. This is our reward. It would diminish if our compassionate actions did not produce the results we wanted them to produce. This shows that it is really an anxiousness for our egos that we have, not a patient, humble enthusiasm for the good. It is ourselves we are serving and not the suffering ones toward whom we act compassionately. If we understood that the good can exist even if we do not help it along, then we could will compassion single-mindedly.

Doing what is good to feed our pride, Kierkegaard states, is a "higher deception" (63). It does not seem to be motivated falsely, because our active involvement in the service of the good makes it look very much as if we are genuinely willing the good. People mistakenly think we are genuinely willing the good because we appear so concerned to see the good come. And we are deceived in the same way.

Self-forgetfulness

Heschel tells a story to illustrate what we must do to avoid contaminating our worship of God with self-worship.

> A disciple of the Kotzker complained to his master that he was unable to worship God without becoming aware of his pride. "Is there a way of praying that prevents the self from intruding?" he asked.
>
> "Have you ever met a wolf while walking alone in the forest?"
>
> "I have," he answered.
>
> "What was on your mind at that moment?"
>
> "Fear. Nothing but fear, and the need to escape."
>
> "You see," replied the Kotzker, "at that moment you were afraid without being self-conscious or aware of your fear. It is in this way that we must worship God."[6]

The key idea in this story is self-forgetfulness. It has two elements plus a causal relation. The first element is focusing

6. Ibid., 95.

our full awareness on something outside ourselves, the second is not being aware of ourselves, and the causal relation is that the first is the cause of the second. In Heschel's story, the Kotzker's disciple directed his fear entirely toward the wolf and as a result had no awareness of the fear. What the Kotzker wanted his disciple to see was that when we worship God in the same way we fear a wolf, the self will not intrude in our worship. Kierkegaard might have put the point by saying that wholly willing the good makes us unmindful of the fact that *we* are doing so.

The idea here is that to will the good single-mindedly we must not notice that we are willing it. Once we do so, we will be tempted to appear good in order to savor our goodness, in which case we no longer are willing the good. We are feeding street people so we can say to ourselves, "*I* am doing something good for them." What we can notice without jeopardizing a single-minded willing of the good is the need of street people for encouragement. We can picture their faces and their ragged clothes. We can even imagine ourselves talking to them. But we cannot let the thought that *we* are willing the good slip into our consciousness. That would allow self-assertion to be what moves us instead of the goodness.

We need to be careful here, though. It is certainly legitimate to savor goodness. What is not legitimate is to pursue goodness so that we can indulge ourselves in our savoring. That would be like doing the good in order to congratulate ourselves for delighting in it. What we need, instead, is a pure and simple delight in the good. With it, we would take pleasure in doing the good, but we would not do the good to get the pleasure.

WILLING ONLY TO A CERTAIN DEGREE

Not Enough

In addition to willing the good self-forgetfully, we must also will it to the highest degree we can. If we do not do this, competing desires, while not destroying the willing, may diminish it. We would then have a different obstacle to willing the good single-mindedly. Kierkegaard calls this obstacle willing "the good only to a certain degree" (64).

This barrier differs from the first three because in them there is only the appearance of willing the good. We think we are willing the good, but our real motives are public admiration, fear of disapproval, or self-admiration. So we are in a state of illusion. The "two wills" in these cases are thinking that we will the good, on the one hand, and really willing something else, on the other. Francois Mauriac put it precisely in *Vipers' Tangle*. Louis, the hateful father who realizes his true motives as he nears death, writes in his diary, "I have always been mistaken about the object of my desires. We do not know what we desire. We do not love what we think we love."[7]

In willing the good only to a certain degree, however, we really will the good. Nor is there any illusion about this—we are right in believing that we will it. What makes willing the good only to a certain degree a case of having two wills is that we also will something else, which pulls us away from willing the good. It is not that we love solely (and thus falsely) for the sake of public recognition, but that we love truly while also desiring recognition. The desire for recognition stands

---

7. Francois Mauriac, *Vipers' Tangle*, trans. Warre B. Wells (Garden City, NY: Doubleday and Co., 1957), 167.

alongside of and not behind the love. And this fact weakens the love. If Louis had loved to a certain degree instead of illusorily, he might have written, "I loved my daughters, but not enough, I now realize, for I also loved money."

One significant form that willing the good only to a certain degree takes in Christian contexts, Kierkegaard observes, occurs when we quickly blaze for the good (69). What happens is that we become gripped with "*a feeling for the good*, a vivid feeling" (68). We might hear a moving sermon or homily on God's love and be "quickly moved, easily prompted to dissolve in emotion" (68). As we listen to a psalm being read, we might burst with gratitude for the good God has given us. Our sense of right and wrong may flare up when we learn about social injustice. We might instantaneously become contrite while listening to a fellow Christian's account of her experience of God's forgiveness. Compassion may burn in us as we hear how infant girls in India are abandoned.

There is no illusion about the reality of these. The compassion and gratitude are real. But they are not real enough. That is, they are not settled and stable. We lose their intensity minutes later. And with this loss, their power to cause us to act compassionately is also lost.

What we feel in these cases (if we reflect on the matter) is impotence. We are helpless, unable to put our desire for the good into motion. We sit on our couches thinking of the hunger of the homeless but cannot get up to make them sandwiches. It is not that we do not want to aid them. We do. And it is not that our desire to aid them has an ulterior motive. It is pure. No self-admiration infects it. But it is also weak. It cannot overcome the comfort of sitting on the couch.

To will the good single-mindedly, Kierkegaard is telling us, we need to do so with a "collected mind," "steadfast diligence," and our "best powers" (67). And to do this, our willing must be unrelenting. It cannot exist only during flare-ups that rapidly subside.

The Allure of Imagination

Nor can it exist only in reflection or contemplation. When we contemplate the good, it is "very inviting, but when [we are] to start out on the road, everything is changed" (74). The good no longer is so attractive. As in flare-ups, it loses its power to move us.

What happens in contemplation of the good is that we forget about the realities associated with being virtuous. We forget the offensive smell that strikes us when we stand too close to street people. We do not remember that sometimes they accept our sandwiches and move on without saying a word, or are not always pleasant to talk to. This forgetting is what makes us see the good so clearly. If we thought of the smell, the vision would fade. And this shows that the vision is only a partial willing of the good. It is real, to be sure, but, like a flare-up, is weak. If it were a full willing, we would take the vision and work it into our actions, gradually but steadily.

Consider a more common case. We picture ourselves listening to a friend in distress. We are a model of patience, and our listening helps the friend regain control of her life, we imagine. Perhaps she gets over suicidal feelings or works through grief. We do not, however, consider the wrenching selflessness we must expend in order to listen well. To be a catalyst for our friend's restoration, we cannot talk about our own distress or our own bouts of depression. We must attend only to her distress. And this is a good deal harder than imagination lets on. When our vision of a good confronts this reality, it diminishes.

An indication, then, that our willing is weak is the presence of imaginings of this sort. We think of good projects and how fine it will be when they are done. We imagine ourselves being patient under duress; we picture ourselves smiling kindly to strangers who have anxious looks on their faces. "The lazy person always has an inordinate imagination," Kierkegaard writes (73).

What leads us astray in both imaginings and flare-ups for the good is feeling. It "enraptures" us, blocking out the self-sacrifice we need to carry through acts of compassion. It blinds us to the realities involved in actually being good listeners. Having said this, though, we must not suppose that the remedy is to get rid of the feeling. For, as Kierkegaard puts it, "immediate feeling is certainly the first, is the vital force; in it is life" (71). Feeling is what moves us to action and what gives spark to otherwise lifeless activity. The remedy, rather, is to remove the blindness from the feeling. That is, "it must be cleansed of selfishness" (71). We must not let its intensity obstruct the stale smell of a street person or the selflessness needed for true listening. When we guard feeling in this way, it becomes stable. It outlasts our imaginings and holds firm despite adverse conditions.

There is something else about imagining that we must note. Though we are not deceived about the reality of the willing, we almost always are deceived about its power and extent. We think that the good we are willing in imagination is strong, when in fact it is weak. We think it extends to real life, when in fact it is limited to our imagination. And these deceptions are what make imagining so alluring. For we like to think of ourselves as possessing an unreserved commitment to goodness.

These deceptions arise easily. If we are part of a religious community, we feel acutely the expectation to live up to our ideals. And we really want to do so. So we picture ourselves acting in ways our community would admire. (The drive to be admired becomes part of the mix.) We savor the thought that we are earnest in our devotion to goodness. (Perhaps self-admiration enters in as well.) But this thought does not notice the difference between imagination and reality, and we do not suspect that our earnestness exists only in imagination. Only later, when the earnestness of imagination confronts the earnestness required by reality, do we become aware of the deception. This discovery does not prevent us from falling back into the deception, however, for we remain desperate to regard ourselves as willing the good. Even though willing the good only to a certain degree contains a real willing of the good, it "is perhaps sometimes just as incurable" as the other kinds, Kierkegaard notes (65).

One might think that we could prevent the deception in willing the good only to a certain degree by avoiding reflecting, by actually loving, for example, instead of simply imagining love. This does, indeed, sound like an effective cure. After all, it is the love, not its imagining, that counts. The trouble, however, is that the imagining creeps in without our knowing that it does. We are carried away by its deception unaware. So what we need is both actual love and reflection. We need to be conscious of what our minds are doing—of what *we* are doing in our minds—so as to root out the deception. We need more reflection, Kierkegaard asserts, not less.

The Charm of Busyness

Busyness, however, prevents us from reflecting on ourselves. "In busyness there *is neither the time nor the tranquillity* . . . to gain any deeper knowledge of oneself" (67). When we are busy, we are constantly preoccupied. We do not notice the secret motives that drive us. We are unaware of the clever ways we convince ourselves that we are pretty good people, worthy of wide admiration. We do not check to see whether anything—the busyness itself even—is undermining our single-minded willing.

Busyness also prevents us from reflecting on the good. "In the midst of busyness there is neither time nor tranquillity for the quiet transparency that teaches equality" (70). Equality for Kierkegaard is essential to willing the good single-mindedly. He is not referring to political equality, legal equality, or equal rights and opportunities. What he is referring to is an attitude of nonsuperiority and noninferiority. When we have this attitude, we do not think of ourselves as better than others because of our accomplishments or position in society. We do not compare ourselves to others, favorably for us and unfavorably for them. Nor do we think of ourselves as inferior to others because we have fewer accomplishments or less public recognition. This would invariably lead to resentment, which is as much an indication of our desire for admiration and status as is the attitude that we are superior.

Kierkegaard's point is that busyness keeps us from reflecting on what the good requires. We are so occupied with getting ahead or with getting through the day that we do not think about what we need to will the good single-mindedly.

Busyness has other effects as well. It keeps us from looking at others from the standpoint of eternity. What matters in busyness is success and getting ahead, so when we observe others from the standpoint of busyness, willing the good single-mindedly is far from our thoughts. "In the busy life, in all the dealings from morning to night, it is not such a scrupulous matter whether a person completely wills the good" (66). It would in fact seem petty to a busy person to ask her whether she single-mindedly desires to be compassionate ("timid and miserable pettymindedness" [65]). This would not be pertinent to her aims, which have nothing of the eternal in them.

Busyness also makes us impatient to get rewards for our good. "The person who wills the good in truth must above all not be busy but must in quiet patience leave everything up to the good itself, what reward he is to have, what he is to accomplish" (97). With busyness, we pounce on some reward we think we should have for willing the good. We also impatiently decide what our willing the good should accomplish. Instead of quietly letting the good have its own way in its own time, allowing it to give us a due reward when it deems fit and to produce its results instead of ours, we anxiously rush into rewards and results. This rushing is a sign that our commitment to the good needs to be stronger.

Because busyness does these things, it represents for Kierkegaard all that is alien to the eternal. From the standpoint of eternity, what counts is the good, not getting ahead. The person with the eternal in her heart wants to know her motives regardless of their frightfulness. She keeps faith and hope and love in the forefront of her attention. She does not assess others' importance simply from the standpoint of how active they are. She waits patiently for the good, not rushing it along so as to be the one who succeeds in it.

Busyness, however, attracts us. "This busyness is indeed like a spell" (66). It draws us in, first captivating us and then trapping us. Kierkegaard alludes to its addictive power. "How sad to note how its power grows with the increasing buzzing, how the spell spreads, seeks to trap the earlier prey so that childhood or youth are scarcely granted the stillness, the remoteness, in which the eternal attains a divine growth" (66). One of the characteristics of addiction is that we constantly engage in the behavior to which we are addicted. Another is that we are powerless to stop our addictive behavior, at least not without extra effort or intervention. Both of these characteristics are true of busyness. If we watch ourselves for awhile, we will notice that we are constantly moving. We rarely sit still, and when we do, we instantly find something to occupy us. Our minds, too, are scarcely ever quiet; they are preoccupied with a thousand matters. We might say, "I must reflect on the eternal," or "I have to figure out what I really want in life." And perhaps we do—for a quarter of a minute. Three weeks pass, and we notice that we have kept on the move, reflecting neither on our inner lives nor on the good. It is as if something is driving us on. Pascal declares, "All our life passes in this way."[8] An impartial observer might suggest that we are enslaved.

Why do we find busyness so irresistible? Kierkegaard gives several reasons. One is that busyness is so common and

---

8. Pascal, *Pensées*, trans. A. J. Krailsheimer (Baltimore: Penguin Books, 1995), sec. 139, 40.

so widely approved. "Everywhere the busy person also has common agreement against" those who would point out the busy person's busyness (68). The presence of busyness is "like poisonous fumes over the fields, like the hosts of grasshoppers over Egypt, so excuses and the hosts of them become a general plague" (68). General approval, of course, motivates us. We like to be acting in ways everyone else will admire.

Busyness also makes us successful. By our "indefatigable busyness" we become "prosperous" (76). Constant work gets us ahead, advances our reputation, perhaps makes us wealthy. If we want these more than we want the good, we will do the work and forget the good.

Last, busyness is a means of evasion. By it we evade both self-knowledge and knowledge of the good. Kierkegaard uses the idea of distraction to make this point. In busyness we have "a distracted mind" (67). We keep our minds active so that we can distract ourselves from seeing the envy and avarice that motivate us. We also keep our minds active so that we can distract ourselves from a clear vision of the good.

The fascinating point Kierkegaard is making is that busyness is not just something that prevents self-knowledge and reflection on the good, but is something that we actively use to prevent these. Busyness is not an obstruction that happens to be in the way of reflecting on ourselves and on the good, but an obstruction we create. The reason this is fascinating is that it suggests that our busyness comes from resistance. We are busy because we resist the good. And this is fascinating because it means that willing the good only to a certain degree, of which busyness is an indication, is also a result of resistance. Kierkegaard's "defiance" is operative here. We are unwilling to understand either the nature of sin or goodness, so we busy ourselves with distractions.

Of course, willing the good only to a certain degree also involves some amount of willing the good. And if this is true, then in willing the good only to a certain degree we have another manifestation of the basic split in human nature. We are genuinely attracted to the good, yet resist it as well.

Oddly, however, Kierkegaard states that willing the good only to a certain degree "does not have the stubbornness of that earlier double-mindedness" (65), that is, the dividedness that comes from desiring reward, fearing punishment, and serving oneself. The question to ask about this statement is, If there is no resistance to the good, then why is there not full commitment to it? It would seem natural to explain the partial commitment by means of the resistance. If unwillingness, or resistance, is rock bottom in understanding the source of sin, as Kierkegaard believes, then it would explain partial commitment as well. Perhaps what he means by the above statement is that willing the good only to a certain degree does not consist entirely of obstinacy. "Its good side is that it nevertheless weakly wills the good" (65). It would then be a case of really willing the good and, because of its weakness, resisting it as well. The resistance would not be total, but would, like the commitment, be partial. This, I believe, is the proper way to think of willing the good only to a certain degree.

By Your Fruits You Shall Know Yourself

As we have seen, Kierkegaard has said that in our imaginings we can think we are fully committed to the good when in fact we are only half-committed. "Alas, contemplation and the moment of contemplation, despite all its clarity, easily conceal an illusion" (72). How, then, can we distinguish between a full commitment to the good and a half commitment? One answer Kierkegaard gives is that we can check our actions to see whether they conform to what we think we are fully committed to: "Is it not truly the only demonstration of someone's having a conviction that his own life expresses it in action?" (69).

Consider two people, both of whom believe in a loving Providence who employs people as means to aid those who suffer. The first one has a keen sense of the presence of such a Providence and is overflowing with a feeling of love and goodness. He may even be bursting with gratitude for the good he has received. But let us suppose that he does not respond to a sufferer whom he encounters. He has changed his mood when the sufferer appears, and is impatient to be doing something of his own. By contrast, the second believer does respond to the sufferer. It is clear, says Kierkegaard, which one has the full conviction and which one does not. That the second person acts as he does shows that he has a conviction that is strong enough to move him. "But it totally escapes the double-minded person that in the very moment when he thinks that faith is victorious in him he contradicts this conviction in action" (69). His inaction shows that his faith lacks motivating power.

We must not think, though, that action is the only way to discover the strength of inner conviction. Surely Kierkegaard's assertion that action is the "only demonstration" of conviction is too strong (69). In spite of the fact that our inner perceptions can be mistaken, it does not follow that they all are mistaken. We can trust some of them, many of them, even, to tell us that others are deceptive. This, after all, is what we do for outer perceptions, such as sight, so why should it not be the same for inner ones? Kierkegaard in fact relies on his own insightful inner perceptions throughout *Purity of Heart*. His aim is to get us to see what he sees. This clearly presumes that he believes that we can trust what we see. So there are in reality two ways to discover the strength of inner convictions: action and introspection. And these two ways interact. It occurs to us to compare our actions with our convictions. We do, and find a discrepancy. So we go back to the convictions and find only half-commitments instead of full ones. Kierkegaard does not discuss the complexities of this interaction, nor does he even mention it. It is enough for him to point out that we need to inspect our actions, since, as he no doubt perceives, we are loathe to do so.

We should not suppose, either, that action is always right in what it tells us about ourselves. Two people may go through the motions that devout persons normally go through. They may sing hymns in church with enthusiasm, kneel at the altar, and talk fervently of things of faith. Yet one may be motivated unconsciously by the need for approval. Her actions would not be a proof at all of the strength of inner conviction. Kierkegaard is aware of this, too. His example of the person who loves solely for money illustrates this possibility, as do his later examples of those who act in religious ways because they are absorbed in the religious "crowd." So again things are much more complex than a simple, "Look at your actions." As Kierkegaard might point out, however, we cannot use this complexity as a dodge to evade discovering our half-commitments. The clear fact is that action and introspection do reveal truths about ourselves. We should not let the possibility of their not always being reliable prevent us from ever using them. If we did, we would be erecting yet another barrier to willing the good single-mindedly.

3

The Price of Willing One Thing

COMMITMENT

WILLING THE good single-mindedly means being willing "to do everything for the good" (79). This does not mean that we must be willing to do any good thing, for people have different capabilities: "the good can indeed require the most diverse things of different people" (79). Does it mean that everything we do should be done for the sake of the good? If it does, being willing to do everything for the good would mean treating everything we do as being in the service of the good. Nothing would be neutral. Some thinkers have believed, on the contrary, that some of what we do, such as tossing leaves about or blowing bubbles, does not matter one way or the other so far as goodness is concerned. This moral neutrality could exist, they say, even though we should in general adopt a standpoint of moral seriousness toward life. Kierkegaard does not address this controversy. Both sides, in fact, are consistent with everything he says. It might be that we should regard everything we do as being in the service of the good, including picking up stray sticks, or it might be that some actions are morally neutral. We do not, fortunately, need to decide which of these views he holds, for what he means by being willing to do everything for the good sidesteps these claims.

To say that we should be willing to do everything for the good means that we should "*will, in the decision, to be and to remain with the good*" (79). In different words, we should be constantly willing to do the good. We should be in a state of readiness to do good things, always open to what is good, even if some of what we do is morally neutral.

Several features of this willing deserve highlighting. One is its constancy. This contrasts with the short-lived character of flare-ups for the good that characterize willing the good only to a certain degree. The principal difficulty with flare-ups is that their intensity cannot endure. No one, in fact, can remain on a high for very long, no matter what kind it is. The "high-minded moment" (80) dies down. The captivating "feeling for the good" (68) subsides. If being committed to the good consisted just of these high points, we would possess little such commitment, for only a miniscule portion of our lives consists of high points. To be a real commitment, our willing must stay with us. A real willing of the good is not the same as an intense one.

A person who really wills the good also "has plenty of time for the good" (80). If we genuinely want to do the good, we will have time for it. And if we do not want to do the good, or want to do it only half seriously, we will never have enough time for it. We will be too busy, both in the sense of having too much else to do and in Kierkegaard's sense of using our activities as a diversion from the good. The case is like anything else we want to do. If, say, we like to knit, we will find time for it, no matter how busy we otherwise are. But if we let our other activities prevent us from knitting, our commitment to it is not at the highest level.

Those who are committed to the good, Kierkegaard continues, take no notice of what their social status is. The reason for this is that eternity does not recognize the distinction between high and low status. What matters in eternity is whether we have truly willed the good, and this is something that both those at the top and those at the bottom can do. Those at the top can disregard the "importance" of what they do and attend only to their willing; equally, those at the bottom can disregard the "insignificance" of what they do and focus only on their willing. There is, accordingly, a leveling that takes place when those at different social levels become committed to the good.

The impulse of people at all levels, however, is to compare. When those with a high social status do something good, they tend to think of it as having more value than what those with a low social status do. And when those with a low social status do something good, they tend to think of it as having less value than what those with a high social status do. From the standpoint of eternity, both comparisons are irrelevant. They are, in fact, injurious. For they undermine real willing of the good. If we think of the good we do as having significance because we have a high social status, we possess pride, and if we think of our good as being insignificant because we have a low social status, we may possess resentment and envy.

Our commitment to the good, then, must remain steady, it must be open to action, and it must be free of all comparisons. Kierkegaard no doubt refers to these as "prices" of willing one thing because they are so extraordinarily difficult to maintain. He states, though, that the good "must be purchased at any price" (87). And he adds that "unconditionally everything must be given up and sold in order to buy it" (87).

THE EXPOSURE OF EVASIONS

Swarms of Excuses and Deception

When we give an excuse, Kierkegaard says, we know the good, yet resist it. We may not at the time think of ourselves as resisting the good, but this is because we do not want to know what we are doing. Later, our conscience finds us out. It says to us, "Do you remember that time.... You knew very well in your heart, *and so did I*, what was required of you, but you shirked" (86).

We might say, "It is too risky to go sandwiching in gang territory. I might be shot or get mugged or catch tuberculosis when I talk to street people there. We shouldn't, after all, throw away all caution." And indeed we should not. But recklessness is not our only option where risk is involved. We may exercise reasonable caution. In nearly every situation involving risk, we can imagine ways of reducing it. If we do not even try to imagine these ways, we are using risk as an excuse not to do the good. The issue then becomes whether or not we really want to do the good. When we perceive that this is the issue, the excuse loses its force. We come to see that from the standpoint of eternity we need to take reasonable risks in doing the good rather than never to do the good so as to avoid all risk.

Perhaps we continue: "I do not have the strength to risk everything this way" (84). Here the excuse trades on two senses of "everything." We may not have enough strength to risk everything that it is possible for anyone to risk. But this does not mean we have no strength. We certainly have some strength. This means that we can take some amount of risk—an amount that matches our strength. When we do, we would be "risking everything that we can." We are not, after all, required to take more risk than we can handle. If, then, we give the excuse that we do not have enough strength to risk everything in the first sense, we are evading using all the strength we do have. Besides, if we sincerely venture out in the service of the good not knowing whether we will be able to handle the risk, we will receive strength simply by virtue of making the sincere venture.

Sometimes we think, "The little bit I can do amounts to nothing" (84). Perhaps we become discouraged at the little that we accomplish compared to what overall needs to be done. So we stop what we have been doing, and the next time an opportunity comes, we don't even try. The excuse in this case is thinking that the good we do must be distinguished. If it is not, we think, then what we do is not worth doing at all. In thinking this, we forget that eternity values every bit that is done. "The slightest bread of charity in the service of the good is infinitely more blessed than to be the most powerful one outside it" (83). It is, to be sure, very difficult to keep conscious of this perspective, because society values visible accomplishment much more than it does crumbs. Still, we are responsible for letting society's values influence us.

With deceptions, Kierkegaard says, we present ourselves to others as better than we know ourselves to be. We cannot let them know what our inner lives are like. So we gather around ourselves friends whom we believe love the good. Ostensibly, our aim is to advance the good together, but really we want to be admired for our industry for the good.

Our intention in these deceptions is the same as it is for excuses—to evade the good. We do so not overtly, but secretly, and not in the worst way possible, but in what seems to us innocuous ways. We are not "totally satisfied with the good's meager reward," so we try to "earn a little on the side—by going around a little on the side" (87). To go around the good a little on the side is, of course, still to go around it.

To these excuses and deceptions we could add numerous others. To describe them all would be to engage in "shadow-boxing"—fighting the air (85). We are, Kierkegaard seems to be telling us, masses of evasions. This is not a very happy way to view ourselves, and we may be inclined to reject it because it is so dark. But Kierkegaard is asking us to look at ourselves without any preconceptions. What we will find, he believes, is two things—numerous evasions, but also a desire to uncover them so as to root them out. We cleverly evade doing the good, but just as cleverly discover that we evade.

A Treacherous Friend

The message of *Purity of Heart* is that the real obstacles in the spiritual life are half-hidden evasions, ulterior motives, and half-commitments, not obvious and fully visible enemies. This contrast is made plain in a passing remark about doubt in Kierkegaard's discourse, "Every Good and Every Perfect Gift Is from Above." "Doubt is sly and guileful, not at all loud-mouthed and defiant, as it is sometimes proclaimed to be; it is unassuming and crafty, not brash and presumptuous."[1] To

---

1. Soren Kierkegaard, *Eighteen Upbuilding Discourses*, edited and translated by Howard V. Hong and Edna H. Hong (Princeton, NJ: Princeton University Press, 1990), 41.

this he adds, "and the more unassuming it is, the more dangerous it is."[2] The dangerous enemies to doing the good, he is saying, are those we cannot easily detect.

Resisting these unassuming enemies requires different tactics than resisting the brash ones. To the latter we respond with direct resistance and outright battle. To the former, we need to respond with clever detection. This difference in tactics is not, of course, quite this simple, for fighting brash enemies requires cleverness, and uncovering half-hidden evasions requires as much courage and strength of will as fighting battles. Nevertheless, the difference is significant. If we think the only way to deal with enemies in the spiritual life is to do battle with them, we are likely not to notice some of the enemies. And this means that they may well control us.

The stance, then, that Kierkegaard recommends in *Purity of Heart* is self-suspicion. We need to distrust our motives. But this is not a malicious distrust. In malicious distrust, we look for unsavory motives that discredit us. We end up with the belief that we are unworthy—thoroughly and totally lacking in value. Kierkegaard is not recommending that we adopt this attitude toward ourselves. The self-hate it involves would undermine faith instead of purifying it. He thinks of self-suspicion, rather, as an element of faith. "Earnestness," which he regards as essential to faith, "is precisely this kind of honest distrust of oneself, to treat oneself as a suspicious character."[3] The distrust is honest because it wants to remove excuses and deceptions, not insidiously use them to degrade ourselves or to evade the good further. Faith earnestly desires a cessation of resistance to the good. For this it needs knowledge of the

2. Ibid., 41.
3. Kierkegaard, *For Self-Examination*, 44.

tactics and intricacies of resistance. Perhaps, then, we can call this nonmalicious self-suspicion, "curative suspicion."

Curative suspicion "uses sagacity *against evasions*" (94). Although we easily discern the nature of evasions when we observe them in others or read about them, we do not easily see our own evasions. We might, for example, perceive that letting oneself be absorbed into a crowd is a way of avoiding having real faith, yet not notice that we are absorbed in a crowd. What we need is clever investigation. We have to act toward ourselves with the same deftness a spy who follows suspected thieves uses. He hides himself from them or makes himself appear like a normal traveler. To do these well he must possess a high level of ingenuity.

The self-investigator must also rely a good deal on memory. It is nearly impossible to reflect on our motives while we are acting on them. That would dilute our attention to what we are doing and produce an intolerable doubleness. What is needed is quiet reflection on past motives.

A clever memory notices that it was really a bit of bragging that time we mentioned an accomplishment to someone. Memory detects our craving for admiration for a project we recently finished; it uncovers the subtle influence of the crowd on what we thought was an uninfluenced decision for the good; it reminds us of the time we shrank back from committing ourselves to the good. Memory pays us numerous visits: "Do you remember how you thought you were being compassionate? That was not your only motive then. You also wanted your friends to notice."

It is not just these evasive motives that memory recalls, else we are likely to end up with malicious self-suspicion. A good-willing cleverness also uses memory to remind us of the good we have done. Memory recalls the time we followed through on a resolution; it brings to mind our steady convictions; it recollects the occasions we have acted selflessly without regard for others' admiration (if it can do so without inducing self-admiration); it remembers the times we felt attracted to the good. On a good day, memory sits down beside us: "You have loved well and you have given what you could."[4]

A good-willing cleverness, in addition, uses memory to keep the eternal in mind. If busyness is not to blot out our sense of eternity, we must remember what we discovered in a quiet moment. We must keep the beatitudes in the forefront of our consciousness, continually remind ourselves of the need for gratitude, and recall our most recent encounter with grace or goodness.

If, then, we want to will the good single-mindedly, we will become "a friend, a lover of recollection" (94). We will cultivate it, knowing that in doing so we are cultivating eternity. In eternity, in fact, we will recall all—the evasions and the good. Memory there will be our companion. In cultivating memory now, consequently, we are beginning to open in this life what will be fully open in eternity.

By now it should be apparent that cleverness is a treacherous friend. We need it to will the good, yet it betrays us into evading the good. Put the other way around, it seduces us into excuses and deceptions, yet we must have it to uncover this seduction. "Sagacity is . . . misused internally

---

4. St. Thérèse of Lisieux writes of her early childhood, "How happy I was at that age. I was beginning to enjoy life and I felt the attraction of goodness." *The Autobiography of Saint Thérèse of Lisieux: The Story of a Soul*, trans. John Beevers (New York: Image Books, 1957), 27.

to seek evasions, but the good person uses sagacity specifically against evasions so that in the decision he might be and remain with the good" (120).

The same is true of self-suspicion. Turning our attention inward can make us more self-centered instead of less self-centered. If we constantly analyze our feelings to see how pure they are, we are likely to miss the good altogether. If memory has only us in its mirror, we will not see anyone else. We will not observe their distress, nor will we know about their delights.

Self-suspicion can also make us morose—light-heartedness and gaiety are not its hallmarks. Although we can handle a bit of moroseness now and then, a little often turns into a lot, and a lot undermines our perceptions of goodness and beauty. With these gone, we lose the delight in goodness that is central to a good-willing life. If we are to keep self-suspicion from undermining this delight, we must consciously remind ourselves that our aim in being suspicious of our motives is to will the good. And we must deliberately curtail self-suspicion on occasions when it is appropriate to cultivate delight.

That self-suspicion is treacherous suggests that it too must be treated with suspicion. It must be balanced with other significant elements of a good-willing life. This is the sort of point that Kierkegaard could have made, but did not. I shall return to it in the last chapter.

4

What Then Must I Do?

ACT DECISIVELY

LISTENING TO a devotional talk or reading a devotional book has its own hazards. One is that we can easily respond by critiquing the talk or book instead of willing the good; another is that we can evade actually willing the good by focusing on understanding what willing the good is. Kierkegaard is not the first to point out these hazards. What distinguishes Kierkegaard's treatment is his description of the subtle ways these evasions operate on us and his emphasis on their power over us. We fall prey to them without knowing that we do; we admire a speaker's eloquence without wondering whether we are willing the good; we clearly perceive the difference between understanding what is good and actually doing it, yet continue to focus on the former instead of the latter.

Kierkegaard uses an analogy to illustrate how we should regard one who gives a devotional talk. Consider a play. The actors rightly expect admiration, and the audience gives it. If, however, we were to regard a devotional speaker as being like an actor, we would be missing the point of what she is trying to do, which is to inspire her listeners to will the good. The proper attitude toward such a speaker is to think of her as a prompter offstage, and the right way to regard ourselves is as the actors to whom the prompter is whispering lines. The prompter tries to be as inconspicuous as possible and wishes not to be noticed. The actors want only to act; they do not pass judgment on the prompter.

Our proclivity to regard a spiritual speaker as an actor, however, is often more than we can resist. We admire the eloquence of the speaking; we notice the way in which the speaker moves easily from point to point; we say to ourselves, "There is thought and depth here." Or we observe the speaker's lack of organization and her inability to make her thoughts clear to us, remarking later, perhaps with a bit of grumbling, that we did not get anything out of the talk. The point is not that we should never admire eloquence, depth, and clarity or never lament their absence. It is that we use these to evade willing the good, which is the aim of our listening.

The evasion involved in substituting understanding for willing is one of Kierkegaard's favorites, and he never tires of pointing it out in other works. In *Purity of Heart*, he simply says, "the understandableness of this discourse and the listener's understanding are still not the true earnestness" (122). In *Concluding Unscientific Postscript*, this contrast between understanding and earnestness is identified with the contrast between objectivity and subjectivity. Since there is no automatic transition from being objective to being subjective, it is possible to be the former without being the latter. In that case, we will miss the most important thing of all. The highest task, Kierkegaard says, is "to become subjective."[1]

---

1. Soren Kierkegaard, *Concluding Unscientific Postscript to Philosophical Fragments*, edited and translated by Howard V. Hong and Edna H. Hong (Princeton, NJ: Princeton University Press, 1992), Vol. 1, 163.

One of the examples Kierkegaard uses to illustrate the difference between being objective and being subjective is the attitude we can take toward immortality. If we think of immortality as "something in general," we are thinking of it objectively and impersonally. It makes no difference to what we do of an afternoon or to what life projects we adopt. It does not even exist for us. What, indeed, is something in general? If, however, we come to think of immortality as something we participate in, then our stance toward it has become subjective. "The existing subject asks not about immortality in general, because a phantom such as that does not exist at all, but about his immortality."[2] The subjective person wonders, "How does immortality transform [my] life.... He asks how he, existing, is to conduct himself in expressing his immortality."[3]

The same is true of death. If we think of death as something in general, we are being objective. We are thinking of death with detachment, as if it affects only someone else. But, says Kierkegaard, "if the task is to become subjective, then for the individual subject to think [of] death is not at all some such thing in general but is an act."[4] We start living as if we will die next week; we picture ourselves being 79 looking back at our whole lives.

Why does Kierkegaard emphasize earnestness and subjectivity so much? The historical answer is that he was writing to a state church which he believed to be filled with passionless objectivity. He thus conceived himself as a missionary to those who thought of themselves as Christians. But why did Kierkegaard think earnestness and subjectivity

2. Ibid., 174.
3. Ibid., 175–77.
4. Ibid., 169.

were so important? The answer to this is that he thought of faith as consisting of these. "Faith," he declares, "is indeed the highest passion of subjectivity."[5] And, of course, faith is necessary if one is to become a Christian. If all that we have is understanding and objectivity, then we are still pagan. "The one who has objective Christianity and nothing else is *eo ipso* [precisely thereby] a pagan, because Christianity is precisely a matter of spirit and of subjectivity and of inwardness."[6] He is not saying that Christianity contains no objectivity or that it is only subjectivity. What he is saying is that with only understanding and no earnestness ("objective Christianity and nothing else") we will not have faith.

Kierkegaard also stresses the power of objectivity to undermine subjectivity. "In this objectivity one loses that infinite, personal, impassioned interestedness, which is the condition of faith."[7] In different words, when we immerse ourselves in understanding Christianity, we are likely to forget that the point is to be a Christian. Often, in fact, we use the understanding to evade real faith. Not wanting to resist faith openly, we do so covertly, using understanding as a blind behind which we hide. We tell ourselves that understanding is good. (It is, indeed, good.) We discover significant theological truths, gain important insights into how they apply to our lives, and feel that we have made a meaningful gain. (We have.) But we let our insights obstruct earnestness.

The way Kierkegaard puts all this in *Purity of Heart* is to say that we may come to understand the subtleties of our evasive tactics, but that is not enough. We need actually to stop

5. Ibid., 132.
6. Ibid., 43.
7. Ibid., 29.

evading the good and to start willing it. This is Kierkegaard's first answer to the question, "What then must I do?"

LIVE AS AN INDIVIDUAL

His second answer is that we need to be individuals. In this we find the central category, not only of *Purity of Heart*, but of all of Kierkegaard's writings. In *Concluding Unscientific Postscript*, he writes that "to be a single individual . . . is a human being's only true and highest significance."[8] Elsewhere he states that "from the Christian point of view, [being an individual] is the decisive category" and that with this category "the cause of Christianity stands or falls."[9] Not to be an individual, Kierkegaard writes in *Purity of Heart*, is "the most pernicious of all evasions" (128).

To see what Kierkegaard meant by being an individual, we need to exercise interpretive care. The most natural sense of this phrase, though it fits some of what Kierkegaard says, does not correspond to the sense he says is required to will the good single-mindedly. The most natural way to interpret "being an individual" is to think of it as meaning "being different from others." To be an individual in this sense is to act differently, believe differently, and have different attitudes from everyone else, or at least from those with whom one associates. Kierkegaard makes a number of statements that lead one to believe that this is what he means by being an individual. He says, for example, that we can know we are doing the

8. Ibid., 149.

9. Soren Kierkegaard, *The Point of View*, edited and translated by Howard V. Hong and Edna H. Hong (Princeton, NJ: Princeton University Press, 1998), 121, 122.

right thing if we do the opposite of what "the crowd" judges to be right (136). The crowd's ridicule tells us that we are on the right path (136), and its judgment on us is a sign that we are truly individuals (135–36). Kierkegaard's negative attitude toward crowds reinforces this nonconformity conception of being an individual. "The bigger the crowd, the more likely that what it praises is foolishness" (133). "It is not the nature of truth to please a light-minded crowd immediately—and basically it never does that" (133). "The crowd seems to be shouting mockingly at God" (134).

Perhaps Kierkegaard had this attitude toward "multitudes" because he himself was ridiculed by the press and the public during one segment of his life. Perhaps, too, he distrusted crowds because he viewed the Danish church of his day—a Christian multitude—as having lost genuine faith. To those in these groups Kierkegaard no doubt wanted to say, "Be different. Don't conform to mindless public opinion or lifeless religion. Become an individual."

However, if this is all Kierkegaard meant by being an individual, he would not have told us what is necessary for single-mindedly willing the good. For we can easily imagine a multitude of like-minded people, each of whom passionately pursues the good. A group of individuals can have the same beliefs and act in the same ways while single-mindedly willing the good. Kierkegaard recognizes this possibility when he says that we can "sympathetically give heed to people and events" while at the same time being individuals (131). This means that we can be individuals even though we are like everyone else in a crowd. It is not, therefore, the first sense of being an individual—being different from the crowd—that is necessary for willing the good, but another sense. This other sense is what Kierkegaard is referring to when he declares that we cannot be Christians unless we are individuals. He has a good deal to say about this other sense of being an individual in *Purity of Heart*, though at times he mixes it somewhat indiscriminately with remarks about being an individual in the first sense.

The key idea in being an individual in the second sense is being fully responsible to God. "Each human being, as a single individual, must account for himself to God" (127). The trouble with the crowd here is not that it is wrong, as it is in the first sense of being an individual, but that we use the crowd to evade responsibility. We hide in the crowd "to avoid God's inspection" of us as individuals (128). This sense of being an individual is the one that is required for purity of heart, for we cannot single-mindedly will the good if we are evading responsibility for doing so. Let us unpack this crucial sense by contrasting it with what Kierkegaard says about hiding in the crowd.

When we hide in a crowd, we identify with it not simply by virtue of having similar beliefs and attitudes, but in a way that involves giving up control of our beliefs and attitudes. We let the crowd control them. Doing so means that we actually become the crowd in a certain sense—the crowd lives our lives for us; we do not live them ourselves. Kierkegaard expresses this condition by saying that we are characterized by "externality" (148). We are not ourselves, but are "external persons." We are in a kind of "oblivion" (134), as if we are nothing—*we* do not act, feel, or believe. The crowd does these for us. Kathleen Norris captures this condition nicely with respect to celebrities: "All too often, romantic love and fanatic devotion to celebrities are an attempt to escape the self, to ask another to *be* your self because the burden has become too much for you."[10]

Earlier, Kierkegaard drew an analogy to cheering to illustrate the seductive power of the crowd. We can use the same analogy to illustrate what it is like to be an external person hiding in the crowd. Kierkegaard quotes Plato: "There where the people come together in a great crowd, in the assemblies, in the theaters, in the camps or wherever else there is a gathering of the crowd, and there where with loud uproar they censure some of the things that are said and done and praise others, but in both cases with excessive cries and clamor and clapping of hands, there where even the rocks and the place where they are assembled echo the noise and repeat twofold the tumult of the praise and the censure—how would it be possible that there a young man's heart, as the saying is, would begin to throb?" (95–96).[11] Kierkegaard responds to this question by asserting that our heart should, indeed, throb if we are to will the good. But, he hints, there are two kinds of throbbing. The kind necessary to willing the good has "the fresh vitality of youth"; our heart beats in this way when we act as an individual (96). When, however, we are seduced by a cheering crowd, our throbbing heart becomes external; it is not our own. We so identify with the crowd's excitement that our own excitement is hollow—there is only an inner emptiness corresponding to it.

If, now, we were to ask what it feels like to be hidden in the crowd in this way, the answer would be that it doesn't feel like anything at all, at least not at the time we are hiding. Our

10. Kathleen Norris, *Amazing Grace: A Vocabulary of Faith* (New York: Riverhead Books, 1998), 90.

11. Quoted from Plato, *The Republic*, 492B–C.

identification with the crowd's cheering undermines awareness of it. It is only later that we notice the externality and oblivion that are present in the identification. By contrast, if we are in control of our inner excitement, and we consciously choose to cheer with the crowd, we are aware of what we are doing. It is not externality and oblivion we would then notice, but individuality and responsibility.

The important question for Kierkegaard, then, is whether we are conscious of being individuals. He repeatedly asks, "Are you now living, my listener, in such a way that you are clearly and eternally aware of being a single individual?" And he declares, "This consciousness [of being an individual] is the fundamental condition for willing one thing in truth" (127). The question is not, "Are we individuals?" To this the answer is yes, in one sense we all are—we are responsible for what we do despite our attempts to evade responsibility. "Ultimately the action and the responsibility are yours alone as the single individual" (131). The real question is whether we are aware of our responsibility. For if we are not, we do not own our virtue. Our convictions are not really ours. Kierkegaard's point is that owning our actions, consciously taking responsibility for them, is necessary for them to have worth. If we are crowd persons, our virtue, no matter how laudatory, and our convictions, no matter how true and significant, have no worth. This is because they are not really ours. Living as an individual, then, involves being aware of our responsibility for our virtues and convictions. It is not just having the responsibility. We have that even if we are not aware that we have it.

It is evident, accordingly, that Kierkegaard is not recommending that we isolate ourselves from multitudes. He is only recommending that consciousness of being an individual should "penetrate [our] life relationships" (137). "You are not asked," he continues, "to withdraw from life, from an honorable occupation, from a happy domestic life—on the contrary, that awareness will support and transfigure and illuminate your conduct in the relationships of life" (137). If we are married, we may go to confession with our spouses, but it is as individuals that we confess (151). We may have intimate relationships with others, but we have an "even more intimate relationship," one in which we as individuals relate ourselves to ourselves before God (129). We may even be part of a group of Christians, just as Christ's disciples formed themselves into a cohesive group. The twelve certainly constituted a crowd, but not, says Kierkegaard, "in the sense that the thesis as I have presented it would become false."[12] His thesis is that the crowd should not become "the authority for what truth is,"[13] not that we should never be part of one. Being an individual, then, is not the same as being isolated. If Kierkegaard sometimes sounds as if it is, that is due partly to his negative assessment of crowds, especially the church in Denmark, and partly to his putting so much emphasis on being an individual. When one puts emphasis on an idea, one is always subject to misunderstanding.

Why did Kierkegaard put so much emphasis on being an individual? Why did he declare that to be "hidden in the crowd, to want, as it were, to avoid God's inspection of oneself as a single individual" is "the most pernicious of all evasions"? (128). Aren't the barriers to willing one thing he described earlier—reward, fear of punishment, egocentric service of the good, and willing the good only to a certain degree—equally

12. Kierkegaard, *The Point of View*, 126.
13. Ibid., 126.

effective ways of evading God? What is so unique about hiding in a crowd?

This question is also pertinent to later existentialists who focus on hiding in crowds. Friedrich Nietzsche's criticisms of the herd instinct, Martin Heidegger's analysis of falling into "the they," and Jean-Paul Sartre's descriptions of bad faith are all reminiscent of Kierkegaard's diatribes against using the crowd to hide from God. Although Kierkegaard does not give an explicit answer to the question, several things he says allow us to reconstruct an answer.

The first truth about hiding in crowds is that it is alluring. "Number tempts," Kierkegaard writes (133). It tempts because at a fundamental level we do not want to will the good. Instead of blatantly and brashly saying "No," however, we do so under cover of the crowd, thinking that we can conceal our resistance. We do, after all, also want to will the good, so we do not want our resistance to it to appear obvious. That is, we do not want our conscience to find us out. Nor do we want God to notice. Like Adam, we hide. It is easier, we think, not to be seen when we are an anonymous member of a crowd than when we are alone.

In addition, we are continually surrounded by crowds. Our workplace contains a crowd; our circle of acquaintances consists of a crowd; so do the organizations to which we belong; the church is one as well. Whenever, in fact, we associate with one or two others, we are coming into contact with the makings of a crowd. The cheering in each of these is not so obvious as it is at a stadium, but it is there nonetheless and we feel it. Number tempts wherever there is number. "Where there are many there are externality and comparison and indulgence and excusing and evasions!" (148). It does not matter, either, whether the many are religious or secular. Both are just as alluring.

Fear also moves us to engross ourselves in crowds. "Why, indeed, does a person run to join the crowd unless he is frightened!" (136–37). Identifying with a crowd, Kierkegaard is saying, alleviates our fear. What fear?—the fear of being an individual. In escaping into the crowd, we "cowardly avoid being the single individual."[14] This fear is actually more than fear; it is terror—a fear so fierce that we shrink in panic and dread. Kierkegaard has discovered what he believes is a rock-bottom drive in human nature—the terror of being an individual—and what he thinks we do to satisfy the drive—lose ourselves in crowds. "The crowd is indeed always the strongest" (132), so it is nearly impossible to resist identifying with it.

Ernest Becker has made Kierkegaard's analysis of hiding in crowds one of the central themes in his magisterial *The Denial of Death*. He says that what lies behind nearly all that we do is the need to believe that we have eternal significance. Death undermines this significance. It ends all the projects we have pursued, topples the monuments we have erected, severs us from our dear possessions. To face these truths head-on, Becker states, we have to do so alone—no one else can confront our death for us. We are, of course, fearful of this confrontation. So we identify with others—a celebrity, a group of like-minded people, a whole culture even. They become a shelter for us. Indeed, they become us, or what comes to the same thing, we become them. To escape the fear of death, then, we hand over ourselves to someone else. "The most terrifying burden of the creature is to be isolated, which is what happens in individuation: one separates himself out

14. Ibid., 108.

of the herd. This move exposes the person to the sense of being completely crushed and annihilated because he sticks out so much, has to carry so much in himself."[15] Becker calls Kierkegaard's description of hiding in crowds a "breathtakingly penetrating ... analysis of the human condition."[16]

The allure of hiding in crowds, the ubiquity of crowds, and the terror of sticking out all explain why Kierkegaard focused on being an individual. For him we cannot pursue eternity single-mindedly unless we come to grips with our propensity to hide in crowds. It is clear, then, that the stakes are high—the highest one can imagine. For when we hide in a crowd, we are setting our eternal destiny the wrong way. But in being an individual, we are setting our destiny the right way.

The right way to live is as if even now we were in eternity. "In eternity you will look around in vain for the crowd" (132). We will, of course, then be part of a vast multitude that sings and dances directly in God's presence. But we will not be using this multitude to hide from God. We will, rather, conceive of ourselves as being alone with God, for that is what we actually will be. In particular, we will not be comparing ourselves to anyone else ("I am dancing before the Lord more wonderfully than my neighbor"). We will not become external persons by losing ourselves unconsciously in others. We will not make excuses for our indifference or lack of compassion. We will not evade the good or deceptively regard ourselves as virtuous. We will, in sum, possess the highest possible attraction to the good. No desire for reward or ego enlargement will contaminate this attraction. We will be this way in

---

15. Ernest Becker, *The Denial of Death* (New York: The Free Press, 1973), 171. See also Chapter 5, "The Psychoanalyst Kierkegaard," 67–92.

16. Ibid., 68.

eternity because then there will be nothing between us and God—no crowd, no excuses, no distractions. To will the good single-mindedly now, Kierkegaard declares, we must import the eternal into the temporal.

We must also possess an array of virtues. In the prayer with which Kierkegaard both begins and ends *Purity of Heart*, he mentions some of these: wisdom, sincerity, perseverance, concentration, resolution, and confidence. I shall say something about two of these.

"May you give in repentance the bold confidence to will again one thing" (7, 154). Without having read *Purity of Heart*, one is likely to find this a surprising petition. Why should willing one thing require bold confidence? Confidence is needed where uncertainty, risk, and danger are involved, and willing one thing does not seem to entail any of these. As we have seen, though, Kierkegaard's reason for including this request in his prayer stems from his assertion that willing one thing demands being an individual. And the very thought of being an individual brings fear and terror to us—we must own our resistance to the good. To do so, we have to relinquish the consolation that the crowd's strength imparts to us.

What Kierkegaard is implying here is that confidence—and its cousin courage—are central virtues in the spiritual life. They are central because we need them if we are to will the good single-mindedly, which is itself of the highest significance. The centrality of confidence and courage is worth calling to mind from time to time, for they are rarely mentioned as vital spiritual attributes. We are more inclined to think they are reserved for those occasions in which we must confront a difficult coworker or ask a friend for forgiveness for a misdeed. If Kierkegaard is right, however, confidence and courage are more pervasive virtues than we might suppose, needed before we step out the front door for the day.

"When everything is going well, give the perseverance to will one thing" (7, 154). Kierkegaard is assuming in this petition that we cannot obtain purity of heart with a quick decision or even with a single resolute effort of the will. It must be worked at, wrestled with, struggled over. This too may be surprising, for Kierkegaard stresses the need to choose and make commitments. The thing to keep in mind, however, is that he also believes in the flawed nature of the will. The will resists the good. It is not a neutral entity, capable of choosing the good in the same way we choose to have blueberries for dessert instead of rhubarb pie. This resistance to the good has become habitual. We instinctively want to hide in a crowd whenever we encounter one. We gravitate toward self-congratulation whenever we are reminded of the good we have done. And these habits are hard to break. Sometimes, in fact, they are like addictions, nearly impossible to escape without assistance or grace. The difficulty in excising our dividedness comes through subtly yet clearly in Kierkegaard's rich descriptions of our evasions and ulterior motives. If we are alert, we will infer, with Kierkegaard, that purity of heart must be gained slowly and honestly (74).

We might also be tempted to infer that it is impossible to have purity of heart in this life. Here, however, Kierkegaard seems ambivalent. Given all that he says about illusion and subterranean motives, we might think he was skeptical about achieving purity of heart. At the same time, the aim of *Purity of Heart* is to evoke genuine penitence, which appears to presuppose that the author thought such penitence possible. Kierkegaard never discusses the issue, systematically or in passing. So I will end this chapter with a quote that displays both skepticism and hope. Perhaps this dual stance is a fitting response to our dividedness. "And this is my faith, that however much confusion and evil and contemptibleness there can be in human beings as soon as they become the irresponsible and unrepentant 'public,' 'crowd,' etc.—there is just as much truth and goodness and lovableness in them when one can get them as single individuals."[17]

---

17. Kierkegaard, *The Point of View*, 10–11.

5

Kierkegaardian Faith

I WANT now to reflect on prominent themes in *Purity of Heart*. What important insights about human nature does Kierkegaard give us? Are crowds as bad as Kierkegaard seems to think? To what extent should one's Christian faith be Kierkegaardian?

LOST INNOCENCE

Inner Conflict

Perhaps the theme that leaps out at one the most in *Purity of Heart* is that we are divided. The assumption behind Kierkegaard's descriptions of ulterior motives is that we want to rid ourselves of them so as to be wholly and cleanly good. Yet if Kierkegaard's descriptions are right, they show that we also want merely to appear good and not actually to be good. We are both attracted to goodness and resist it.

Kierkegaard is surely right about this dividedness. When we inspect our wants and desires, we find that they fall into two categories. We genuinely want goodness. A number of inner phenomena confirm this. We delight when we observe what we take to be unfeigned kindness. We are disgusted when we discover that a man loves, or appears to love, a woman merely for the status it brings him. We like to hear stories in which people perform some noble action from a noble motive. We recognize the goodness that is depicted in accounts of the life of Jesus and are drawn to that goodness. We want our motives to be untarnished.

We also genuinely do not want goodness. This, too, is confirmed by a number of inner phenomena. We avoid thinking about ulterior motives, hiding from the thought that ours may be stained. We gravitate to newspaper stories about violence and other crimes, usually more than we do to stories about acts of kindness, which seem boring and uninteresting to us. We choose to believe the worst about people. We like being praised so that we can feel our egos inflating. We secretly delight in imagining ourselves using others for gain.

This inner conflict calls to mind a tug-of-war. Imagine a long, thick rope—500 feet long, say, and two inches thick. A hundred people are pulling at each end. They are spread out along the rope, one person every two feet, with a hundred feet between the two groups. Let us suppose, too, that there are people milling about who do not aid or cheer for either group; they are just there. Sometimes, though, these people join the pullers at one or the other end of the rope. In addition, from time to time, some of the people from each end of the rope run to the other end and pull from there. The rope, too, moves back and forth. Because the tug-of-war is taking place on a large plain, there is room at each end of the rope for it to move a long way. Sometimes, perhaps, the rope does not move in either direction.

Something like this haphazard scene is constantly taking place inside us if Kierkegaard's understanding of the inner life is on target. The people pulling on the rope represent our desires and motives. Some of them pull us toward the good, and some pull us in the opposite direction. The direction in which the rope moves represents the direction in which our overall character is headed. That people occasionally change sides on the rope depicts the changing alignment of our desires and motives with respect to the good. The people milling about correspond to neutral desires, the ones that do not seem either to serve the good or to resist it. From time to time, though, some of these neutral desires join with the movement toward or away from the good. The overall scene is a picture of the jumble that is in us, the conflict between our attraction to goodness and our resistance to it. The intensity of the pull may be stronger in some persons than it is in others, but in no one does the rope ever go slack. The pull is real and it is always there.

Clearing the Mist

There is another feature we must add to this picture of our inner life. Over the whole plain on which the tug-of-war is taking place there is a pulsating, cloudlike mist. This mist prevents us from seeing clearly all that is going on. We are able to discern some of the details some of the time and the whole scene some of the time as well. Usually, though, we are not too sure what is happening, unless the mist clears for a bit. Then we are better able to observe both the movements of individuals in the tug-of-war and the tug-of-war as a whole.

Kierkegaard's project in *Purity of Heart* requires, rightly, that this mist be present. There would be no need for him painstakingly to poke around in our inner terrain and communicate his explorations to us if it were clear and perspicuous to everyone. The implication, of course, is that we are largely strangers to ourselves. We rarely know what is lurking behind our surface feelings. We often do not see the place our motives and desires occupy in the larger significance of things. And our ignorance in these matters is mostly self-induced. (The mist somehow is our own doing.) We do not want to know either about our attraction to the good or our resistance to it (though, being divided as we are, we also do want to know about them).

Suppose we ask, "What happens when we clear the mist?" Obviously, we will be able to observe the tug-of-war. We will come to know which of our motives attract us to the good and which resist the good. Something else happens, too. The tug-of-war actually becomes more intense. Our gazing at it makes the participants pull harder. We, of course, are the participants. So somehow in noticing our own inner conflict, the conflict intensifies. When we see that we are attracted to the good, we find ourselves attracted even more. Likewise, in noticing our resistance, we resist more strongly.

This phenomenon is not unique. When we first realize that we have fallen in love, we are moved to love more ardently. After discovering that what we most want to do with our lives is be a teacher, we invest ourselves in that endeavor more wholeheartedly. When we awake to the fact that we do not like our job, the dislike increases.

There is a risk, then, in clearing the mist. It is that we may never be the same again. Becoming less of a stranger to ourselves not only clarifies our dividedness. It increases it.

The Crucial Struggle in Life

We can add one further element to our tug-of-war scene. Scattered on the field in random locations are other, smaller tugs-of-war. Sometimes the people in these smaller tugs let go of their ropes and start milling about; other times they join the main tug. These smaller tugs-of-war represent other kinds of struggles not involving either the good or resistance to it. These struggles may not last long—they might dissolve or they might become part of the large tug-of-war. In the pulsating mist, all that we see at times is just these smaller struggles. Or we may see them distinctly and the larger one not so distinctly. Then the smaller ones loom larger than they really are.

The truth of the matter is that the struggle to be good is the largest struggle on the field. This is the overriding message that comes through in Kierkegaard's intricate portrayal of motives that undercut our willing the good. It is also the overriding message in Plato's *Republic*. He, too, depicts a strenuous inner conflict, similar in some ways to Kierkegaard's. Near the end of *The Republic,* Socrates remarks, "The struggle to be good rather than bad is important, Glaucon, much more important than people think."[1] One might slip by this observation with merely a blink of the eye. But if one pauses, one will see that it is of the last importance.

---

1. Plato, *The Republic*, trans. G. M. A. Grube, revised by C. D. C. Reeve (Indianapolis: Hackett Publishing Co., 1992), 608B, 279.

The Mystery of Resistance

Let us go a bit further and ask, "What accounts for our inner conflict?" Kierkegaard does not ask this question, but he does employ a concept that suggests an answer. That concept is defiance.

Suppose we ask what is behind one of the motives that undermine our attraction to goodness—self-congratulation, say. We might answer that pride is. Now suppose we ask what motivates pride. We might respond that we are not content with being creatures; we want to be God. If, now, we ask why we want to be God, no answer seems forthcoming. We just do.

The same is true for other motives that diminish our attraction to goodness. Consider envy. We are envious when we resent others' advantages or successes. Why do we feel resentment? Because we feel diminished by their successes. Why do we feel diminished? Because we are not fully open to God's grace. Why that? Here all we can say is "Just because."

What these questions seem to show is that at bottom resistance to goodness has no explanation. We just resist. Pure defiance is part of our make-up.

One way to test this idea is to engage in Kierkegaard-like introspection. When we do, we find that underneath the lure of reward, fear of punishment, and egocentric service to the good, there lies a pure and simple "No." This is, perhaps, one of the most haunting results of actively exploring our motives. Why is there a tug-of-war on the field? There just is—we both do and do not want to be good. Kierkegaard illuminates the complexities of our resistance, but the resistance itself remains a mystery.

A Tangle

Although there is a deliberate "No" within us, it rarely stands out in our consciousness. The motives and desires that stand out are more everyday ones, such as the desire to have a new sweater or car or the desire to succeed in our jobs. Or they are motives that impair single-minded attraction to the good, such as self-congratulation and reward. They can also be desires involved in the seven deadly sins, such as an inordinate desire for food or possessions. When we exhibit greed, for example, we do not typically say to ourselves, "I do not want goodness in my life, so I am going to amass possessions." Or when we climb our ladders of success, we rarely openly declare, "I do not want to be open to God's grace, so I am going to justify myself by my accomplishments." Things are more tangled than that. Our resistance to goodness is woven into the network of our everyday motives in intricate ways.

One way in which defiance intermingles with our other motives is by blinding us to the good-making or good-undermining dimension of them. Goodness thus becomes less of a consideration in what we do and desire. When we allow success to breed self-justification, for example, we do not think of ourselves as resisting goodness. The same is true when we let a materialist mentality become our main focus—we do not think of how goodness connects to the piling up of possessions. This is because we do not want to know how it connects. So in cases when defiance is not directly responsible for misdirected motives, it may be indirectly responsible. The "No" to goodness comes earlier in the chain of events, which makes it harder to detect.

A similar process occurs when our resistance to goodness causes us to be more accommodating to motives that undermine goodness. We become more willing to let ourselves feel diminished by another's success and more willing to say critical things about acquaintances. It does not feel so bad that we are envious or that we judge others.

Blindness and accommodation are so mingled with our desires, emotions, and motives that it is often difficult to discern the presence of defiance. What we have inside us is a hodgepodge of knowing and ignorance, willingness and unwillingness. When Augustine asks, "Who can untie this extremely twisted and tangled knot?"[2] he is referring to this tangled mess. Somewhere in the tangle is a brute "No" to the good. Sometimes it is on the surface. More often it is hidden within the tangle.

Three Ways of Going Wrong

This brute "No" plays a role in another prominent theme that is displayed in Kierkegaard's *Purity of Heart*. One of the questions he is answering is, "How can we go wrong in life?" His answer is, "By not being attracted to the good singlemindedly." In order to place this answer in a wider context, we need to lay out several answers that one could give to the question.

One answer is, "By acting contrary to moral principles." Here the emphasis is on overt actions. When we unjustifiably hurt someone with our words, take up with a friend's spouse, gossip, walk out of stores with unpaid merchandise, cheat on our income taxes, or drive recklessly, we go wrong in this first

2. Augustine, *Confessions*, Book 2, sec. 10, 34.

way. The model here is the criminal, who violates the law. If we go wrong in this way without deserving to land in jail, we are moral criminals.

A second answer is, "By having wrong desires." Here the emphasis is on inner states. When we have a cynical attitude toward others, allow ourselves to enjoy a friend's spouse in our imagination, are greedy for a larger investment package, think of ourselves as superior to uneducated yard workers, or feel resentment when a coworker is publicly rewarded, we go wrong in this second way. The model here is the person who on the outside appears to be a paradigm of virtue, but who on the inside is consumed with hate and loathing. The seven deadly sins are significant examples of this second way of going wrong.

A third answer to the question is, "By failing to have a larger life." Here the emphasis is on exemplifying as many virtues and other goods to the highest degree that we can. When we constantly keep people at bay, exercise little compassion, rarely experience moral beauty, or do not allow ourselves to be loved, we miss the mark in this third way. The model in this way is the person who fails to respond to Jesus' invitation, "I came that they may have life, and have it abundantly" (John 10:10). When we fail to have a larger life, we constrict ourselves. The aim in living life well in this third conception is to expand, to bring a large number of genuine goods into our lives.

We should not think of each of these answers as excluding the others. Rather, each supplements the others. We do, however, tend to focus on the first, neglecting the other two. And we often have little conception of the third.

In which category does Kierkegaard's answer fall? Certainly it does not fall into the first one of acting contrary to moral principles—not being attracted to the good single-mindedly is a matter of motives. It does fit, though, into the second category of having wrong desires. And it also fits into the third category of failing to live a larger life. Kierkegaard is telling us how we miss the good. If the desire for reward motivates us in our contacts with others, we miss out on real connections with them. If we are driven by self-congratulation, we never experience self-forgetful identification either with those who suffer or with those who have joy. If fear of disapproval dominates our relationships, we are not able to let ourselves be loved without regard to our appearances.

Our resistance to the good, Kierkegaard is telling us, is resistance to the larger life eternity offers. We shut down. We do not let the eternal expand us. Our rock-bottom "No" is a simple refusal to be extravagant in goodness. Our recognition of this is truly innocence lost.

On these matters, Kierkegaard perceives clearly. We are divided. Our biggest struggle is to exemplify the good. We simply say "No" to it. Yet we are attracted to the good. And we are invited to let it squeeze out the "No."

SIMPLE SOULS

Must We Be Suspicious of Ourselves?

One of the most conspicuous features of *Purity of Heart* is Kierkegaard's insistence on the need for self-examination. Because of the pervasiveness and hiddenness of motives that undercut our single-minded willing of the good, Kierkegaard appears to be saying, we need continually to be probing our inner lives. The question one is prompted to ask is, "Isn't he putting too much emphasis on introspection?"

There are two angles to this question. I have already mentioned the first in treating self-suspicion as a treacherous friend. Too much self-examination can lead to self-centeredness, and it can also cause one to be morose and depressed. These consequences are more than just possible; they are likely. Without a balance between introspection and action, self-suspicion and self-forgetfulness, constant self-examination tends to turn us away from the good more than it brings us closer to it. There is more to pursuing the good than preparing ourselves for confession.

The second angle to the above question deals with the possibility of not needing any introspection at all. Could there be people who immediately will the good and do not need to probe their inner lives? Must we assume that everyone should be self-suspicious? Why could there not be some people who simply and purely will the good and do not need to look for ulterior motives in themselves?

On the one hand, no one's desires and motives are entirely untainted. Everyone uses others to inflate their own ego and indulges in self-congratulation from time to time. On the other hand, to say that no one ever acts with single-minded motives goes beyond what we know about other people's inner lives. It might be that some people on some occasions immediately will the good. To say otherwise is unsupported by the evidence.

Both of these perspectives are proper, I believe. Although it is likely that most people need a good dose of Kierkegaardian self-suspicion, there may be some who possess a good-willing simplicity. These two perspectives can, in fact, be found in Kierkegaard, though the first is much more prominent. The impression one obtains from working through *Purity of Heart* is that we are all morasses of ulterior motives that need persistent investigation. Yet Kierkegaard explicitly allows for the possibility that there are people who do not need his antidote. Indeed, he seems to think that such people actually exist. "The sagacious person needs to take a lot of time and trouble to understand what the simple person at the joyous prompting of a pious heart feels no need to understand in lengthy detail, because he at once simply understands only the good" (25). He makes a similar reference in *Concluding Unscientific Postscript*: "What is developed here by no means pertains to the simple folk, whom the god will preserve in their lovable simplicity . . . , the simplicity that feels no great need for any other kind of understanding. . . . On the other hand, it does pertain to the person who considers himself to have the ability and the opportunity for deeper inquiry."[3]

The division Kierkegaard sets up is between those who grasp the good simply and at once and those who grasp the good only with the agony of much introspection. The former have a "joyous prompting" toward the good. Their first attraction is to the good, which they instantly will without having to untangle an array of contrary motives. The latter need to identify those motives before they can wholeheartedly will the good. They are lured by them and must struggle with them so as to get past them to the good.

Let us suppose that Kierkegaard is right and that some people do not need his elaborate descriptions of ulterior motives, because they simply and purely will the good. What

3. Kierkegaard, *Concluding Unscientific Postscript*, 170.

should our attitude be toward this fact? Perhaps we should put this question in a more Kierkegaardian way: What should our attitude be toward ourselves? Can we justly think of ourselves as simple souls?

The right answer, the safe answer, is, No, we dare not think of ourselves in this way. We might be mistaken. If we were, then thinking of ourselves as simple would be a dodge to escape having to uncover tainted motives. Our first stance toward ourselves should be an earnest and honest self-distrust. That is what keeps faith alive, at least for those who are not simple souls. But even if we were simple, to think of ourselves as simple would be equally dangerous. It would be like a humble person thinking of herself as humble—doing so would tend to undermine the humility. We would be tempted to congratulate ourselves and think of ourselves as having achieved the pinnacle of virtue. So either way, whether we are simple or whether we are not, we need to beware of regarding ourselves as simple.

A Knowing Simplicity

At the same time, we may, and should, think of ourselves as pursuing simplicity. We should want to be in the position of willing the good immediately without being suspicious of our motives. We should desire to be the kind of person for whom willing the good is an impulse that arises spontaneously and naturally. The aim of self-examination, after all, is to move to a position where we no longer need it.

The simplicity we aim at, however, is not the naive simplicity Kierkegaard seems to have in mind when he refers to simple souls. The naively simple person "feels no need to understand in lengthy detail." She grasps the good without knowing about tangled motives or having to wade through them. The person who is simple in this way does not have the talent for deeper inquiry. The picture we get here is of one who is unable to follow the subtleties of Kierkegaard's descriptions. If she meditates, it is of particular good things—the love of an acquaintance for another, the love of God for her.

This naive simplicity differs from what I shall call a "knowing simplicity." In knowing simplicity, the aim is the same as it is for naive simplicity—to grasp the good instinctively and naturally. But the one with knowing simplicity "needs to take a lot of time and trouble" to achieve this aim. The time is spent in examining motives. The trouble comes from realizing that one is deeply divided, from recognizing tainted motives for what they are, and from wrestling with them so as to gain the good. In short, the person with knowing simplicity knows the ways in which her desires and motives have gone wrong, yet single-mindedly wills the good. She keeps her knowing in the background of her consciousness, and, like the naively simple person, keeps the good in the forefront.

With knowing simplicity, one knows that he is lured by reward and self-congratulation, yet he attends to the good despite this knowledge. He is troubled by the fact that he is not always attracted to the good, but he wills it nevertheless with an unworried and untroubled delight. The fear and trembling provoked by self-suspicion is present, but it is overshadowed by a glad and active attraction to the good.

These two stances toward oneself can also be taken toward others. A child with naive innocence has no knowledge of the shortcomings of the persons to whom she is attached. Her attachment is simple and pure—"immediate," to use Kierkegaard's word. An adult with knowing innocence, however, has knowledge of another's shortcomings, yet looks through that knowledge so as to see the good in the other, as if the shortcomings did not exist. She is aware of truths that the naively innocent person has no inkling of.

Prince Mishkin in Dostoevky's *The Idiot* possesses this knowing innocence toward others. Dostoevsky wrote *The Idiot* in order to depict a "truly beautiful soul." He recognized that such a person would possess something like the innocence of childhood. And he also recognized that once childhood is past, the innocence in it cannot be recaptured, especially if one has worked through searching self-suspicion. What one must do, Dostoevsky was aware, is to work at acquiring a stance that is like that of childhood innocence even though one has lost that innocence. This is the stance that Mishkin has. He sees the beauty and goodness in others naturally and spontaneously in spite of his also having seen their tragedies and darknesses.

INDIVIDUALS WITHIN COMMUNITIES

Do Groups Only Deaden?

Kierkegaard's distrust of crowds is clear and striking, both in *Purity of Heart* and in his other works. Crowds are a source of pseudo-Christianity. They tempt us to hide from God. They undermine our faith and hamper us from taking full responsibility for our lives. In general, crowds divert us from pursuing the eternal.

Kierkegaard softens his reproach by admitting that it is possible to be an individual while being part of a group. Though we must confess as individuals, we may go to the altar and kneel beside others. We can join ourselves in common cause with other people of faith without sacrificing our own individuality. Marriage, that most intimate of "crowds," is also consistent with knowing that we are individuals before God. The consistency comes from the fact that being an individual does not mean being different from others in a crowd, as we saw earlier, but means being accountable to God.

Though the possibility of being an individual while also being part of a crowd is mentioned only parenthetically by Kierkegaard, he does clearly affirm it. At the same time, one has the feeling that he admits it only as a concession. We can be individuals in spite of being in an assemblage, but certainly not because of it. More than this, even, the reader gets the impression that Kierkegaard's principal attitude toward crowds is unwavering suspicion. Nowhere in *Purity of Heart* does Kierkegaard recognize that being in a group can motivate one to become an individual.

The truth is that crowds can both deaden and quicken. They can shield us from true faith, as Kierkegaard so often declares, but they can also promote it. What needs to be added to Kierkegaard's insightful descriptions of ways in which groups lead us astray is the equally significant awareness of ways in which they direct us to the eternal.

Nurturing Individuals in Communities

How can groups prompt one to be an individual? One way that presents itself was practiced by Kierkegaard himself: talking about the means we use to evade responsibility, about the lure of hiding in crowds, and about the need to be wary of becoming a crowd Christian. When a sermon, homily, or discussion deals with these strategies of avoiding being an individual, we are induced to notice them in ourselves. Although analyzing our motives is an individual activity, it is spurred by listening to others talk about nuances of the interior life.

It is also spurred by personal talk about one's inner life. When someone contritely articulates the apathy or envy she is trying to overcome, others often resonate with that. There is something about someone's confession of inner waywardness that prompts listeners to examine their own apathy and envy.

Kierkegaard saw that people in a group tend to pick up the attitudes and stances others in the group have. As we have seen, he pounced on negative stances, such as pretending to be persons of faith, which provokes others to pretend as well. If, however, we turn this around, we get a more positive view of faith communities. When others are honest with themselves, we are stimulated to be honest with ourselves.

Self-honesty is also stimulated in a group when those in the group exhibit unconditional positive regard for others in the group. People in such a group accept others in the group regardless of their successes or failures. This means that people in the group are less likely to pretend that they are persons of faith who have little trouble being good. The basic attitude in such a group is that people in it regard themselves as needing each other to sustain their faith and to pursue the eternal.

One of the most significant ways in which those in a nurturing community exhibit positive regard for others in the community is by active listening. In active listening, the listener displays both interest and understanding. When conversations turn toward hurts and wounds, this listening shows acceptance and identification with the wounds. Listeners accept admissions of doubts and insecurities graciously, without intimidating glances. They look straight into another's eyes with kindness. The one listened to feels that she is affirmed for her own sake and not judged for her admissions.

All of these—talking about motives, displaying self-honesty, showing positive regard, listening—move one to be a Kierkegaardian individual. We can, then, embrace groups and welcome the good ways they shape us. Kierkegaard, however, was too wary of them.

CALLS FROM ETERNITY

Too Much Awareness of Sin?

Early in *Purity of Heart*, Kierkegaard refers to two emissaries of eternity: regret and repentance. We need these, he says, if we are to will the good single-mindedly. They goad us into uncovering ways in which we have not done so. They make us sensitive to matters of eternity and turn us from the temporal.

The question to ask is whether regret and repentance are the only emissaries eternity has. This is not just a peripheral concern; it strikes at the core of Kierkegaard's overall approach to Christianity. The dominant motif of *Purity of Heart* is that we need to become aware of our waywardness so that we can repent of it. This is a principal theme, too, in the Lutheran tradition of which Kierkegaard is a part, and indeed, in many other traditions in Christendom as well. Awareness of sin in these traditions is the first and foremost way of approaching God. Regret and repentance fit well into this overall stance.

The significant task *Purity of Heart* has accomplished for these traditions is to analyze the subtle and shrewd ways we resist the good. It has demonstrated that the depth of our resistance is more than we normally grasp or are willing to admit. It has also shown that the focus of our sin-awareness energies should be on inner ways of going wrong and not just outer ones. Motives count for everything in our pursuit of eternity. *Purity of Heart* drives this point home sharply.

In focusing on these things, though, important as they are, Kierkegaard has perpetuated the notion that regret and repentance are the main avenues of gaining access to God, if not the only avenues. To maintain balance, we must also consider ways in which our attraction to goodness can be heightened. To concentrate on resistance to goodness, even with the aim of rooting it out, is to give undue attention to one of our two rock-bottom drives and not enough attention to the other.

Observing Goodness

One way in which our attraction to goodness can be heightened is by observing and celebrating it in others. When we do so, we are not analyzing our double-mindedness; we are not repenting of self-congratulation or being regretful for using acquaintances for our own enhancement. We are simply and purely delighting in the good.

Kierkegaard, to be sure, writes in ways that prompt one to delight in the good, especially in his other works, such as *Works of Love* and *Eighteen Upbuilding Discourses*. But the occasions on which he does so get lost in a sea of sin-awareness writing. If we take what he writes as an indicator of what he most wants to say, the message that comes through is that awareness of sin is of more significance than observing goodness. To counteract this implicit message, we would have to describe various modes of goodness and the kinds of delight we can have in them with as much sophistication and breadth as Kierkegaard gives to his descriptions of double-mindedness. I am not going to do that here. It is doubtful, indeed, whether anyone can do it well, given that sin is so much easier to explore than goodness. I will, though, indicate a few of the highlights that such an exploration would involve.

The basic idea in observing goodness can be given in a couple of analogies. Imagine that someone is encountering the Grand Canyon or Niagara Falls for the first time. She gasps in awe at its magnificence. Her attention is riveted to the immensity of the spectacle. It is some moments before she can turn away.

Now imagine that someone is sitting at the shore of a large lake on a windy day. There are boulders at the shore and the waves are washing over one of the smaller ones. When they do, they engulf it entirely. Then in receding, they expose it again. Our observer is watching this cycle. For some minutes she gazes at it. Gradually a sense of the beauty of the scene overtakes her. She experiences a certain wonder and awe in the water's washing over the boulder, and the image of its doing so becomes etched in her mind.

In our first picture, the magnificence is immediately evident, and the sense of awe is intense and sharp. In the second picture, the beauty becomes apparent only slowly and quietly, and the awe is calm and tranquil.

These two pictures typify two kinds of reactions we can have to the goodness we observe. In some cases we have an excited exhilaration or an overpowering awe at truly exceptional generosity or risk-taking courage. These are the kinds of cases in which a virtue stands out in a fashion we rarely witness. Perhaps we read about heroic actions or ventures, or hear accounts of sacrificial compassion. It is possible even that we have an acquaintance who has exhibited remarkable grace in vexing circumstances. To these instances of exceptional goodness we can react with the same sort of awe we have when we first glimpse a spectacular natural phenomenon.

These kinds of cases are the ones we first think of when we visualize ourselves reacting with admiration to instances of goodness. But they are merely the more unique and rare cases. Goodness is unmistakably present in countless everyday circumstances, and we can react to it there as well. Though our reaction may sometimes be like that toward the unique cases, more commonly it will be a calm and quiet awe that grows on us instead of arising instantaneously. In either case, we will possess a keen enjoyment of goodness, not in the abstract, but as it is actually exemplified. We will delight in a kindness displayed to another, a smile on the face of one who has been depressed, an act of forgiveness, hospitality to the inept, and compassion to the homeless. We will come to have a warm-hearted wonder when we remember the encouragement someone gave to another and a deep respect for the perseverance and sacrifice of a young mother raising children alone.

If one of our basic drives is attraction to goodness, we will decidedly want to discover both heroic and everyday occurrences of goodness. We will want to become the kind of person who instinctively and naturally notices the good in others. We will develop a thirst for detecting and perceiving it.

Self-forgetful Praise of God

Another way in which our attraction to goodness can be heightened is by delighting in the goodness of God. The idea is the same as in observing goodness in others—we focus not on ourselves but on the beauty and excellence of God.

The distinction between praising God for what God has done for us and praising God solely for God's goodness is exhibited in the Psalms. In some passages, the Psalmist praises God for the benefits God has bestowed on him: "I will extol you, O Lord, for you have drawn me up, and did not let my foes rejoice over me" (Psalm 30:1); "Bless the Lord, O my soul and do not forget all his benefits—who forgives all your iniquity, who heals all your diseases . . . , who satisfies you with good as long as you live" (Psalm 103:2–5). This praise is not selfish, because the Psalmist is not giving it in order to get something in return, nor is he giving it because of self-aggrandizing benefits he has received. The benefits are uniformly good. Nevertheless, the praise is self-directed, because it is prompted by what God has bestowed on the Psalmist.

This self-directedness is absent in other passages from the Psalms: "Sing to the Lord a new song, his praise in the assembly of the faithful" (Psalm 149:1); "How good it is to sing praises to our God; for he is gracious, and a song of praise is fitting" (Psalm 147:1). The Psalmist makes no reference to what God has given to him. He forgets himself and directs his attention solely to God. The reason given for the praise is simply that it is fitting. As with observing goodness in people, we feel fulfilled when we experience this delight in God's goodness, not as the satisfaction of a self-regarding desire, but as the completion of our deep longing for the goodness of the eternal.

We may say, then, that eternity has another emissary, namely, delight. Delight provides an appropriate balance for Kierkegaard's repentance and regret. It draws us out of ourselves, in contrast to the self-directedness of repentance. It gives us a serene contentment, as against the unsettling dissatisfaction of regret. It makes us feel, overall, that life is good, as indeed it is.

Epilogue

It is difficult to read *Purity of Heart* sympathetically and not come away unscathed. Even with a cheery disposition, we are likely to feel distress at the depth of dividedness within. We will ask, "How can I pursue eternity knowing that my deepest devotion is tainted with alien motives?"

Perhaps Kierkegaard would respond that the aim of confession, for which he wrote *Purity of Heart,* is forgiveness. And forgiveness brings release and joy. So beyond the suspicion and tainted motives, beyond the hidden ulterior agendas, there is hope of something better.

Still, this hope may not be enough to dispel our distress, for if Kierkegaard is right about our dividedness, we are highly ambivalent about confession itself and the forgiveness it is supposed to bring.

Perhaps we must end our Kierkegaardian exploration with this thought: the heart of one who pursues the eternal is a strange paradox. It possesses a sense of eternity while at the same time it blunts that sense. It is drawn to humility yet proudly congratulates itself. It loves the good but constantly undermines it. Only by recognizing these paradoxes will we make progress in our journey to the eternal.

Index

Admiration, 20
Augustine, 13, 78
Awareness of sin, 88

Becker, Ernest, 12
Busyness, 37–41

Commitment to the good, 45–48
Comparing, 47
Confession, 3, 94
Confidence, 68–69
Crowds, 59–68, 85–88
    hiding in, 61–63, 64–67

Defiance, 40, 76–77
Dividedness, 12–15, 71–74
    a strange paradox, 94
Divine punishment, 25–26
Dostoevsky's underground person, 8–9

Egocentric service of the good, 28–31
Eleventh hour, 2–3
Eternity's emissaries, 3–4, 88–93
Evasion, 40, 48–50, 56
Excuses, 48–50

Fear-driven goodness, 24–27
Fear of punishment, 23–28
Flare-ups for the good, 33–35, 46

Good-driven fear, 25–28

Heschel, Abraham, 28, 30–31
Hidden self, 5–9
Howling at night, 12, 14

The Idiot, 85
Ignorance of the good, 7–8
Imagination, 34–37
Individuals, 59–64
    in groups, 64, 85–88

Knowing and willing, 7–8
Knowing simplicity, 83–85

Memory, 52–53
Moll Flanders, 27
Moses, Man of the Mountain, 6

Naive simplicity, 83–84
Nurturing community, 86–88

Observing goodness, 54, 89–91

Pascal, 39
Perseverence, 69
Plato, 62, 75
Praising God, 92

Regret, 3–4, 88
Repentance, 3–4, 88
    illusory, 4–5
Resistance to the good, 6, 12–13, 15, 40–41, 65, 69, 72, 76–78, 80

Reward, 18–23

Sandwiching, 28–29, 48
Self-admiration, 28–29
Self-deception, 6, 30, 35–36
Self-forgetfulness, 30–31
Self-suspicion, 51–54, 80–83
    curative, 52
    malicious, 51
    a treacherous friend, 53–54, 81
Simple souls, 81–85
Subjectivity and objectivity, 56–58

Tangled knot, 78
Tests for willing the good single-mindedly, 21–23, 42–44
Tug-of-war, 72–74
Two wills, 12–15

Vipers' Tangle, 32

Willing only to a certain degree, 32–44
Willing the good single-mindedly, 9–11, 15, 16, 22, 31, 34, 37, 45–48, 53, 59, 60, 63

www.ingramcontent.com/pod-product-compliance
Lightning Source LLC
Chambersburg PA
CBHW070510090426
42735CB00012B/2728